Battleground E

Airfields and Airmen
The Channel Coast

Not mine the roar of the raging sea,
Nor the martial roll of drums;
Not mine the rush through the dust or slush
To gather up Glory's crumbs.
But the life I love
Is away up above,
Like a lively lark to sing and soar,
And win fresh fame for the Flying Corps!

Not mine to delve in the dug-out deep
With the gay yet earnest crew;
Not mine to tramp till I get the cramp.
Though I honour the chaps who do!
But mine the delights
Of the aerial heights,
Where 'tis trebly sweet to sing and soar,
And honour the crest of the Flying Corps!

Oh, it's war on land, and war on sea,
And it's warfare everywhere;
But the game that thrills, despite the spills,
Is the conquest of the air!
The sons of earth
May prove their worth,
But it's finer far to sing and soar,
With a heart that's true to the Flying Corps!
Anon

Battleground series:

With the continued expansion of the Battleground Series a **Battleground Series Club** has been formed to benefit the reader. The purpose of the Club is to keep members informed of new titles and to offer many other reader-benefits. Membership is free and by registering an interest you can help us predict print runs and thus assist us in maintaining the quality and prices at their present levels.

Please call the office on 01226 734555, or send your name and address along with a request for more information to:

Battleground Series Club Pen & Sword Books Ltd,
47 Church Street, Barnsley, South Yorkshire S70 2AS

Battleground Europe

Airfields and Airmen
The Channel Coast

Mike O'Connor

Series editor
Nigel Cave

Pen & Sword
MILITARY

I dedicate this to all those people who have generously helped
with photographs, information and given freely of their time
in order to make this series of books possible.

First published in 2005, by
PEN & SWORD MILITARY
an imprint of
Pen & Sword Books Limited
47 Church Street, Barnsley, South Yorkshire S70 2AS

ISBN 1 84415 258 8

The right of Mike O'Connor to be identified as Author
of this Work has been asserted by him in accordance with
the Copyright, Designs and Patents Act 1988.

A CIP catalogue record for this book
is available from the British Library.

Printed and bound in Great Britain by
CPI UK

Pen & Sword Books Ltd incorporates the imprints of
Pen & Sword Aviation, Pen & Sword Maritime, Pen & Sword Military,
Wharncliffe Local History, Pen & Sword Select,
Pen & Sword Military Classics and Leo Cooper.

For a complete list of Pen & Sword titles please contact:
PEN & SWORD BOOKS LIMITED
47 Church Street, Barnsley, South Yorkshire, S70 2AS, England.
E-mail: enquiries@pen-and-sword.co.uk
Website: www.pen-and-sword.co.uk

Cover Painting: By Colin Ashford GAvA. Willy Coppens, Belgium's most successful
fighter pilot, bringing down a kite balloon in his blue Hanriot HD1. See pages 86 and 90

CONTENTS

INTRODUCTION BY SERIES EDITOR

This latest addition to Michael O'Connor's wonderful series of books on the Airmen and Airfields in the Great War lives up to the very high standard of its predecessors. Although I was always very keen to ensure that the RFC and the RAF found a place in the **Battleground Europe** series, and had some idea of how it might be done, I could never have envisaged how successfully Mike has translated the ideas into practice, producing wonderfully informative books on the airmen and so many of the airfields. Excellent photography – modern and archival – and superbly clear maps have made a pilgrimage in the footsteps (if not the flight paths) of these extraordinary men a practical possibility. An important feature is the number of foreign pilots and airmen who have been incorporated into his story – the Germans, the Belgians, the French and the Americans all get plenty of space.

This particular volume is ambitious, as it covers areas mainly outside the centres for Great War battlefield visitors; but Mike has skilfully produced a number of itineraries that go a long way to overcoming this handicap.

The war in the air has a fascination all of its own; the nature of the combat and the stress upon those engaged in it were unique and it allows a rather different form of investigation than for their earth and sea bound comrades in arms. Amongst its features is the scope it allows for concentrated attention upon the individual; for perforce activity in the air involved a very limited number of people. Thus the frequent biographies are poignant, full of detail and often with mementoes of those who survived or of those who served and flew with them.

It has been my fortune to edit a number of books, most recently Colonel Jack Sheldon's very important, **The German Army on the Somme 1914 – 1916.** All of these add to my knowledge of this 'war to end all wars', helping to ensure to a wider public that these young men of both sides are not forgotten as the years pass by. Trying to bring some sense of individuality to the grinding military machine and the horrendous human cost of mass, industrialised warfare has always been a mission for me. Over the recent decades hundreds of books and monographs have tackled this aspect, involving many, many hours of diligent and painstaking research. We are fortunate also with our contemporary military historians who have shown how the system worked and tried to move on from the simple one-liner platitudes that often are served up as considered criticism about the war and its conduct. Without their commentary, we would be without context.

The war in the air is no exception to this, and as Mike makes clear in his acknowledgements, we who write for the series are enormously indebted to these numerous authors for the depth of information that they provide. This book is an important addition to the duty of remembrance: accessible, clear and ensuring that we can find our way to those places – often very out of the way and poorly visited. It offers a practical way to commemorate and honour 'those magnificent men in their flying machines'.

Nigel Cave
Collegio A Rosmini, Rome

ACKNOWLEDGEMENTS

This volume of *Airfields and Airmen* books has only been possible due to the help of Walter Pieters, who supplied all the information for the *Aviation Militaire Belge* (*AMB*) plus the photographs. I recommend his book *Above Flanders' Fields*.

Yet again I am extremely indebted to Alex Imrie for all his help. About a third of the photographs are from his collection.

I would also like to thank Sylvia Menzies of Pen and Sword, who has done yet another splendid job on the book layout.

My next thanks have to go to Jim Davies and Barry Gray. Jim has, as usual, spent considerable time and effort in proof-reading, writing directions and many other tasks for the book, plus flying the aeroplane for the aerial shots. Barry has produced many of the images, spending thankless hours in his darkroom.

I would also like to thank the following: Colin Ashford GAvA for his usual splendid cover illustration; Paul Baillie; Nigel Cave; the staff of the Commonwealth War Graves Commission; Jacques de Ceuninck; N R Cunningham-Reid; Bernard Deneckere; Air Vice-Marshal Peter Dye; Marco Fernández-Sommerau; the German War Graves Commission; the late Hal Giblin; Dorothy Gough; Barry Greenwood; Christine Gregory, latterly of the RAF Museum; Tim Harper; Trevor Henshaw; Phil Jarrett; Jeff Jefford; Jan Keohane of the Fleet Air Arm Museum; Peter Kilduff; Stuart Leslie for his enormous help with photographs; Bob Lynes; Tony Mellor-Ellis; Simon Moody, also latterly of the RAF Museum; Roger Nixon; the staff at Pen and Sword, the staff of the Public Record Office; Keith Rennles; Alex Revell; Ray Rimell; the staff of the *Service Historique de l'Armée del'Air*; William Spencer; Stewart K Taylor; Keith Thomas; Alan Toelle; Alan Wakefield of the Imperial War Museum; Aaron Weaver; Mike Westrop; Brigadier Henry Wilson and Lawrie Woodcock and Greg VanWyngarden;

Every effort has been made to contact the authors of the various books or articles quoted and their copyright is acknowledged.

AUTHOR'S INTRODUCTION

This volume, the fifth in the *Airfields and Airmen* series, covers all the area to the north and west of Ypres with places which could not be included in *Airfields and Airmen: Ypres*. It covers the activities of the Belgian air service, Royal Naval Air Service and the German naval flying units as well as the RFC/RAF.

Cross referencing notes in the text

As the *Airfields and Airmen* series has expanded more points of interest have become interlinked. It has been necessary to include more notes in the text referring the reader to incidents or places in the other books. In order for this not to be intrusive or interrupt the flow of the narrative I have abbreviated where possible. Thus instead of writing, for example, See *Airfields and Airmen: Ypres* page 147, this has now been reduced to *Ypres,* page 147. Also within the text where it refers to other pages in the same volume this has been reduced to (page ?) from (see page ?).

The military background to the area

After the initial advance of the German army through the area and then the so-called 'Race to the Sea', where the opposing forces endeavoured to outflank each other, the military situation settled down to a war of stalemate. This was due in part by the fact that the Belgians opened the lock gates at Nieuport in October 1914 and flooded large areas around the River Yser creating an almost impregnable defence line. The Belgian army played little part in the rest of the war until the last great Allied offensive in the late summer of 1918. This was not a reflection on either their courage or determination but purely of logistics. Left with a tiny corner of their country the Belgians did not have the manpower resources to sustain large numbers of casualties. A large battle such as Third Ypres or the Somme would have left them without an army.

THE GUIDE

There have been many guides to the various battlefields of the Western Front, some of them extremely detailed, but there have not been any concerning the flying aspect. Using old photographs, maps and contemporary accounts I visited old aerodrome sites and was amazed how little many of them had changed. You can hold up an old photograph of some of them and the scene behind today appears only to lack the aeroplanes. In fact many of the farms associated with these aerodromes have probably changed little in two or three hundred years.

For the military historian most of the First World War has a convenient chronological and geographical sequence in that one can relate how far a battle progressed (or not as the case may be) on a day-by-day basis. The air war unfortunately does not fit into this tidy pattern. Squadrons or flights would take off from one point, have a fight or range an artillery battery at another and casualties would be spread all over the front, on both sides and many miles behind the actual fighting. Casualties from a single air battle might be buried in different cemeteries miles apart.

This guide has attempted to link interesting events and individuals together, into some sort of logical and digestible order, despite the differences in time and geography. The choice of personalities and events is purely my idea of what is interesting. There has always been the glamour of the scout or fighter pilot and the 'aces' and in recent years there has been what I consider an unhealthy obsession with trying to discover 'who shot down whom'. This at best is a risky past-time, taking into account the confused nature of an air battle, the fallibility of human memory and the marked absence of German records. The air war was not just about aces but involved all the mundane tasks of photography, reconnaissance, artillery ranging, bombing, tank co-operation, infantry co-operation, supply dropping and all the myriad tasks that enabled the Allied armies to win the war. To concentrate on just one aspect of the aerial battle does not do justice to the rest.

However in a book of this kind one cannot ignore the 'aces' theme, though I use the information of 'who got who' advisedly and would hope that I have presented a reasonably balanced picture of what the first air war was like.

The Commonwealth War Graves Commission

The Commission never fails to impress me and any praise for them is too little. They care for my grandfather (and my mother) and maintain the beautiful cemeteries with what seems a ridiculously small workforce. I have trouble keeping my garden under control and yet they maintain acres of manicured grass and lovely flower beds to perfection, with a mere handful of staff.

I would urge all visitors to the cemeteries to record their comments in the Visitors Book, for this not only shows the Commission and its staff that their work is appreciated but it also keeps alive the memory of the thousands of servicemen buried there.

HOW THE GUIDE WORKS

At the beginning of the guide is a map of the entire area covered by this volume. On it are marked the major towns and the aerodromes, with an overlap so that the reader can also relate places to features that appear in other volumes. Many of the place names in this part of Belgium are now spelt in Flemish instead of French, as they were in the First World War. In the text I have used the old spellings but for directions from one place to another the modern form is used.

THE TOURS AND DIRECTIONS

The guide has three tours for ease of presentation but there is no compulsion for the visitor to follow these and the reader can visit individual sites at random. Each tour has its own map with the locations of all the points to be visited, plus most of the places that are mentioned in the text. However, if you cannot find a certain point or feature refer to the first overall map in the book. All maps and aerodrome diagrams are aligned with north at the top. All are to scale but not necessarily the same scale.

There are directions from one site to another. Much of the Channel coast area is heavily industrialized, similar to the Ypres volume and some directions become a little complex. I would strongly suggest that paying a few euros for the green IGN 1:100,000 scale map covering the area is a sound investment.

AERODROMES

For all aerodrome entries there is an associated plan, with present day buildings annotated. This should enable the reader to orientate himself. Also noted are the locations of some of the buildings and other features that once stood there. On the plans there are arrows that are aligned with present day photographs, which explain more fully the layout and views you can expect to see. The arrow has a number alongside it referring to the relevant photograph. Some of the aerodromes have disappeared under housing estates and industrial complexes and require a little imagination on the part of the visitor. Many of the points of interest that you can visit were established on farms or near chateaux. They are of interest to you and me but please remember that these are private residences and they do not like hordes of visitors crossing their property any more than you would. Please respect their privacy and use your discretion.

CEMETERIES

In each cemetery entry I have given the Commonwealth War Graves reference number. In *Airfields and Airmen: Arras* I wrote that production of the old yellow Michelin maps with the War Graves over-printing had ceased and a new booklet was in the offing. I am pleased to say that this has happened. The new handbook, entitled *Cemeteries & Memorials in Belgium and Northern France*, utilizes the yellow 1:200,000 Michelin maps but each cemetery now has its own individual number. In addition there are alphabetical and numerical listings. It is an excellent production and an invaluable guide to the battlefield visitor.

At each cemetery the pertinent grave numbers are given, so that the visitor has a starting point for not only the individual involved but the section of associated text. I would suggest that you view the cemetery register and locate the grave to be visited, as the orientation of some cemeteries can be confusing to start with.

TABLE OF MAPS

1. A Map of the Channel Coast Area
2. A Map of the Eastern Area
3. A Map of the Central Area
4. A Map of the Western Area

THE DEVELOPMENT OF MILITARY FLYING

Great Britain

Early Days

Military experiments with balloons began at Woolwich Arsenal in 1878 and a balloon section participated in the Aldershot manoeuvres of 1880 and 1882. These were judged a success with the result that a Balloon Equipment Store was set up at Woolwich by the Royal Engineers to manufacture balloons, instruct in ballooning and serve as a Depot.

In 1883 the Store was transferred to the Royal Engineers Depot at Chatham and was renamed the Balloon School and Factory.

During Sir Charles Warren's expedition to Bechuanaland in 1884 three balloons were employed with a force of two officers and fifteen NCOs and other ranks. After this episode, however, little official interest was displayed and it was only the efforts of a few enlightened officers which kept military ballooning alive. For example, experiments in observing gun fire were carried out, mainly with captive balloons. In 1890 a balloon section was introduced into the army as a part of the Royal Engineers and two years later the centre of balloon work was moved to Aldershot. During the Boer War in 1899 four sections were employed and carried out useful work in directing artillery fire and observation, despite unfavourable conditions and not a little prejudice. In 1905 a better site at South Farnborough was chosen and this evolved into what became the Royal Aircraft Factory (later re-titled the Royal Aircraft Establishment to avoid confusion with the Royal Air Force) and the site of the famous Farnborough air shows. In 1911 the Air Battalion of the Royal Engineers was formed and the Balloon School at Farnborough became No.1 Company and No.2 Company, with aeroplanes, moved to Larkhill in Wiltshire.

The Royal Aircraft Factory

The aeroplane experiments of two aviation pioneers, Lieutenant William Dunne and Mr Samuel Cody, were encouraged by Colonel Capper, superintendent of the balloon factory, despite very meagre financial resources. In September of 1907 the first British army airship, *Nulli Secundus*, flew at the Factory. Cody was involved with this and had been supplying man-carrying kites to the Factory since 1904. The Factory carried out research into all aspects of aeronautics and did much to standardise component parts of aeroplanes. The value of this was demonstrated during the war when a host of furniture and wagon making companies could be subcontracted to manufacture aeroplanes or aeroplane parts. There was criticism from some areas that the Factory was a government monopoly and this came to a head in 1916 with the so-called

'Fokker Scourge' when British losses increased considerably due to obsolete machines. These had been largely products of the Factory. Friction arose as the Factory felt it should supervise and co-ordinate the efforts of the private makers, whilst the independent aeroplane makers feared the paralysing effect of officialdom.

Private enterprise

The British had taken up aviation rather late and were well behind France and Germany. The Royal Aero Club had been formed in 1901 and issued its first Aero Certificate to a qualified pilot, J T C Moore-Brabazon, in March 1910. The first, recognised, powered flight in Britain had been made by Cody in 1908 using a self-built machine, and in 1911 Tom Sopwith had also built his own aircraft, having previously flown mainly French and American designs. He acquired premises at Kingston where during the First World War thousands of his aircraft were built, including the legendary Sopwith Camel. There was no shortage of enthusiasm, though most of the early pioneers were reasonably well to do and were spending their own money. By the beginning of the First World War there was a host of aircraft manufacturers, some of them quite small and many destined not to survive the post-war collapse of the aviation industry. Geoffrey De Havilland built his first machine in 1910 but later that year joined the government Royal Aircraft Factory. The main centre for civil aviation was the motor racing circuit at Brooklands where A V Roe had made his inaugaral flight, though there were other centres like Eastchurch, and Claude Graham White's works at Hendon (now the home of the Royal Air Force Museum).

The Creation of the Royal Flying Corps

The lack of official interest and progress in aviation was continually highlighted by the aviation press and eventually the government was forced to act. A sub-committee of the Imperial Committee of Defence recommended the creation of a British Aeronautical Service and this came into existence on 13 April 1912. It was called the Royal Flying Corps and was to consist of a Military Wing, a Naval Wing and a Central Flying School. The old No.1 Company became No.1 Squadron and No.2 Company became No. 2 Squadron. In theory it was a combined military and naval air service, but in practice it was doomed to failure with split control. The Naval Wing continued to do its own thing, ultimately becoming the separate Royal Naval Air Service (RNAS).

Between 1912 and the outbreak of war the RFC carried out considerable experimental work in co-operation with the army, aerial photography, bombing, wireless telegraphy and photography.

In the army manoeuvres of 1912 each of the two opposing forces were supplied with an RFC squadron. The defending side was able to use air reconnaissance to locate the attacking force, commanded by General Douglas Haig, whilst the cavalry had been unable to do so - and in a fraction of the time. Grierson, commanding the defending force, used aeroplanes for reconnaissance for the rest of the manoeuvres.

The Royal Naval Air Service

The Royal Navy initially showed interest in airships for the protection of trade routes due to the apparent lack of performance and promise of aeroplanes. After a disastrous start, when their first airship broke its back before even flying, interest quietly lapsed. However, in 1911 a patriotic pioneer pilot, Francis McClean, who owned the site of the flying field at Eastchurch on the Isle of Sheppey, offered to loan two of his machines to train four RN officers. George Cockburn, another pioneer pilot, offered to train them free of charge and Short's provided free technical assistance at their factory. Short Brothers had their factory at Battersea but later opened another at Eastchurch and became almost the exclusive supplier of seaplanes to the RNAS. Later in 1911 McClean bought another ten acres at Eastchurch and gave it to the Royal Navy to set up their own flying school. Much experimentation was carried out with wireless, seaplanes and flying aeroplanes from ships. Shortly before the war the Navy revived its interest in airships, ordering several from different manufacturers, including some from Germany, and in January 1914 airships became the exclusive preserve of the Royal Navy. By the beginning of the war the RNAS had established a number of bases round the coast of Britain.

To War

In June 1914 the RFC concentrated all its squadrons at Netheravon. The mornings were given over to trials and experiments and the afternoons to lectures and discussions. Reconnaissance, photography and moving landing grounds were all practised, and plans for mobilization were also formulated. Four days were allowed for this, with a move to France on the sixth day.

War came in August 1914. At its declaration No.2 Squadron made the epic flight down from their base at Montrose in Scotland, and yet 2, 3 and 4 Squadrons were all at Dover by the evening of 12 August, with 5 Squadron arriving two days later. 6 Squadron was given the job of preparing the aerodrome at Dover and some of their personnel made up the numbers of the other squadrons. The squadrons crossed the Channel on the morning of 13 August. There had been meticulous planning for this operation with all the support transport collected at Regents Park and consisting of motor cars and commercial vehicles still in the gaudy colour schemes of their previous owners.

The RFC was a tiny force of 276 officers and 1797 other ranks – about half the size of an infantry brigade. It took to the field with virtually all of its available resources and the aeroplanes left behind were largely worn out or scrap. In command of the RFC was Brigadier General David Henderson, who had fought at Khartoum in 1898 and distinguished himself during the Boer War. He had learned to fly at Brooklands at the grand age of 49 and over the next four years was probably the most influential force on the development of British air power.

The four squadrons collected at Maubeuge on 16 August and for two or three days relatively little happened. On Wednesday 18 August the first historic reconnaissance was flown by P B Joubert de La Ferte, in a Bleriot of 3 Squadron and G W Mapplebeck in a BE2 of 4 Squadron. Both became completely lost in cloud but were able to return later unscathed. The RFC quickly proved its worth and on 22 August large bodies of enemy troops were spotted advancing on the British line. During the retreat from Mons the squadrons moved from field to field, moving in all about ten times in as many days. In particular the RFC spotted von Kluck's attempt to outflank the British Expeditionary Force and the signal was taken personally by Henderson to British Headquarters.

After the Battle of the Marne and the so-called 'Race to the Sea' the RFC moved north with the rest of the British Army and set up headquarters at St Omer, where they soon settled into the pattern that would remain for the rest of the war. With the advent of static trench warfare the style of operation involved mapping enemy trench systems and fortifications, ranging artillery using wireless, photography and bombing. In November 1914 F H Sykes, who was in charge of the RFC at the time, decentralized the RFC and grouped 2 and 3 Squadrons to make 1 Wing, with 5 and 6 Squadrons comprising 2 Wing, each responsible to First and Second Armies respectively.

Expansion

With the massive increase of the British forces on the Western Front there came the last significant change in the RFC structure when, on 30 January 1916, Wings were grouped to make Brigades. A Brigade would consist of a Corps Wing, whose squadrons were dedicated to particular artillery formations in their Army, and an Army Wing with fighter squadrons, whose job was to clear the air of enemy machines and protect the Corps aircraft. By the end of the war a Brigade could have more than two Wings, and as the British army took over more of the line from the French further Brigades were formed to support the newly created Armies. Each was a self-supporting organization with its own Aircraft Park for issuing new machines, its own Kite Balloon Wing and all the other ancillary units such as ammunition columns and lorry parks.

The Royal Air Force

The public outcry about the German air raids on Britain, particularly the daylight aeroplane raids of the summer of 1917, forced the government to completely re-appraise the whole question of the air services. A committee under the great South African statesman Lieutenant General Jan Christian Smuts examined all aspects of air policy and organization. The main feature was to be the establishment of an independent air service by the amalgamation of the RFC and RNAS into a single force, the Royal Air Force, on 1 April 1918. One of the main driving forces during this process was Lieutenant General Sir David Henderson. There was much grumbling from the independent RNAS concerning the loss of their naval terminology and tradition, but nevertheless it worked and many ex-RNAS officers reached the highest ranks of the RAF.

Germany

Zeppelins and balloons

The German experience in many ways was similar to the British, though they utilized airships, particularly the rigid *Zeppelin* type, to a much greater degree.

In 1884 the Prussian Army set up a detachment to examine the use of balloons and by 1901 this had grown to two Companies. Like the RFC they used spherical balloons, both tethered and free, but then moved onto the sausage-shaped kite balloon similar to the observation balloons used in the First War. Even though most of their efforts were directed at airships, in October 1908 the General Staff set up a technical section to observe various areas, including aviation. The War Ministry, bowing to the suggestions of the General Staff, authorised financial help to the most promising of the private aeroplane constructors. A prize of 40,000 marks was put up in 1908 for the first flight by a German aeroplane and this was won in October of that year at Johannisthal near Berlin.

Aeroplane development

The *Albatros Werke* put an aeroplane and a pilot at the disposal of the military, in much the same way as Francis McClean had done with the Royal Navy at Eastchurch, and by March 1911 ten pilots had been trained. As a result of a military commission investigating various types of machines, seven were eventually purchased. At the army manoeuvres of 1911 aeroplanes gained valuable experience but the army was still more concerned with balloons. Fortunately for the Germans the Chief of the General Staff, General von Moltke, was a far-sighted officer and in 1912 proposed detailed plans of how the aviation services should be organized.

The War Ministry was still concerned, however, that the promise of heavier than air flying could suffer a setback and that the flying services were receiving more attention than they should. However these plans did start to come together in October 1913 when *Oberst* von Eberhardt became the first *Inspekteur der Fliegertruppen* on the formation of the office of *Inspektion der Fliegertruppen* (abbreviated to *Idflieg*). Considerable training and expense went in to the *Fliegertruppe* from this date up to mobilization on 1 August 1914.

The German air organisation

At the outbreak of war there were thirty-three *Feldflieger Abteilungen* (field flying companies) with six machines each, with another ten allocated to the fortress towns of Germany, plus twenty-three balloon units and twelve army airships, most of which were unsuitable for operations. Each of the eight German Armies were allocated a balloon unit and one *Feldflieger Abteilung*, with another to each Corps. The airships were kept under the control of Army High Command, but due to a variety of factors their numbers were halved within a month and they were never actually used for reconnaissance in the West. The Army High Command was entitled the *Obersten Heeresleitung*, which was abbreviated *OHL*.

The German air service, like their RFC counterparts, operated a mixed collection of machines, and not until the middle of 1916 did the two-seater units have an aeroplane with a forward firing gun for the pilot and a ring mounted machine gun for the observer at the back. These were designated C-type machines. In addition the Germans were the first to utilise the fixed machine gun synchronised to fire through the propeller. An aircraft equipped with this feature, the single-seater Fokker monoplane, was able to maintain aerial supremacy from mid 1915 until the Spring of 1916.

By March 1915 the number of *Feldflieger Abteilung* had more than doubled and specialist units were being developed. The bomber force was eventually amalgamated into *Kampfgeschwader der Obersten Heeresleitung or Kagohl* (ie *Ka* of the *OHL*) and five of these units were formed.

The first fighter squadrons

Initially the Fokker monoplanes were allocated to two-seater units in twos or threes but for the Battle of Verdun in 1916 they were reorganized into three *Kommandos*. In August 1916 they became *Jagdstaffeln* (hunting squadrons, abbreviated to *Jastas*). Equipped with the new biplane D-type single-seat machines replacing the out-dated E-type monoplanes, and with a strength of a dozen aeroplanes, these *Jastas* were the first true German fighter units. Finally in October the position of *Kommandierenden General der Luftstreitkrafte* (*Kogenluft*) was created and was now responsible for all German flying units (except the German navy and Bavarian ones) including training and reported directly to the Chief of the General Staff of Armies in the Field. This was the formation of the German Army Air Service.

All flying units were re-organised and the old *Feldflieger Abteilung* became *Flieger Abteilung* and the artillery units were re-designated *Flieger Abteilung* (A). The former carried out long range reconnaissance for army headquarters and the latter the duties of infantry co-operation and artillery observation. Units were no longer responsible to individual Corps but allocated to each Army and as such were very similar to the shape and operation of the British Brigade system that had evolved a few months earlier. The head of each Army's flying units was titled *Kommandeur der Flieger* (*Kofl*).

The *Amerikaprogramm*

With the entry of the United States into the war Germany realized that American industrial might would soon be a deciding factor and a decision must be forced before this happened. The flying services embarked on a major expansion, which they called the *Amerikaprogramm*, calling for an increase of forty *Jagdstaffeln* and seventeen *Flieger Abteilung* (A), in addition to massive increases in aircraft production and training. In June 1917 *Jastas* were grouped together into *Jagdgeschwader*, when *Jastas* 4, 6, 10 and 11 combined to form *Jagdgeschwader* 1. The target of forty fighter units was achieved but in practice most were only up to half strength and in the end the two-seater units increased by only six of the projected seventeen, though the strength of some others was increased.

In March 1918 the German army launched its last great offensive to try and obtain a breakthrough before the might of the American forces could become decisive. The use of new tactics and the new reserves, brought from the Eastern Front, very nearly triumphed. Losses in the *Luftstreitkräfte*, or German Air Service, were high.

The End

In June 1918 *Kogenluft* produced another expansion plan but German industry was unable to meet these targets, due to the lack of raw materials. The training of pilots and observers could also not keep up with demand. Finally, the Allied blockade reduced the amount of fuel that German aeroplanes were able to use. At the Armistice on 11 November 1918 the German army had some 280 flying units and a personnel total of about 4,500, which was considerably less than the RAF. Nevertheless, it had been effective in the way it had been employed.

Under the terms of the Armistice the German air service handed over all its fighters and bombers and though some aeroplanes were used in fighting on the Eastern front during 1919 it was officially disbanded in May 1920.

Belgium

Belgium's small size, limited resources and intention to remain neutral in any conflict, all led to meagre beginnings for the Belgian Air Service – the *Aviation Militaire Belge* (*AMB*). Despite this, King Albert was very air minded, and although never a pilot himself, he was flown several times over the lines during the course of the war, although occasionally the pilot responsible had to pretend to misunderstand his requests to go deeper into German Occupied territory!

It was King Albert who had encouraged the setting up of the Military Aviation School in 1911, although its original establishment stood at just five pilots, two mechanics and one carpenter, but no aircraft. And it was the King who presented the school with its first aircraft, when he handed over to them a machine which had been given to him as a gift by Baron de Caters.

Perhaps it is natural that any small organization will have its share of individualists, and the *AMB* seems to have had more than its fair share of innovators. In September 1912, Belgium became the first European country to fit a machine gun to an aeroplane and fire at a ground target (a sheet). The same crew travelled to England in November to repeat the demonstration at Hendon, then at Aldershot, for the benefit of the British Army. Their favourable reception contrasted with the original demonstration in Belgium when they had been castigated for damaging the sheet!

By 1914, there had been some expansion, as four squadrons existed. This increase was not as great as it might seem, however, as each squadron numbered just four Henri Farmans, flown by five pilots and six observers. Ground equipment consisted of five lorries, one for each squadron and another used as a workshop. So at the outbreak of the war, the *AMB* was nothing if not compact and highly mobile.

Belgium had a small aircraft factory which after the occupation became the Military Workshop or depot in Calais. As a result throughout the war the *AMB* was reliant on the French, and, to a lesser extent, on the British to provide its machines. As a result it tended to be given surplus and obsolescent aircraft by its allies, which makes the achievements of its aces all the more remarkable.

The aircraft supply situation was not helped either by the weather. Most of the *AMB*'s aircraft were destroyed on the ground by a violent storm on 13 September 1914, and every one of its aircraft was lost in a hurricane on 28 December. On a day to day basis the weather along the coast was perhaps the worst anywhere on the Western Front, and between February 1915 and November 1918 on 432 out of 1380 days the weather was too bad for any operations to take place at all.

For reasons of limited range and patriotism, most of the operations of the *AMB* were conducted from airfields squeezed into the small portion of Belgium still unoccupied by the Germans. The natural aggression of the pilots, trying to avenge the invasion of their country, had to be tempered with their being such a small number of them that the loss of just one or two would cause significant difference to the crew establishment. The prevailing westerly winds, the bane of Allied pilots, drifted any combat eastwards deeper behind German lines, so prolonged combats were not encouraged. And even if combats were successful, unless the German aircraft came down in Allied territory, or near enough to the front lines to be observed by Allied troops, victory claims were hard to establish.

In February 1916 the first dedicated fighter squadron was formed when Escadrille I became the 1*ère Escadrille de Chasse* equipped with French Nieuport scouts. However, aeroplanes were never numerous and in January 1917 the *AMB* only had thirty-nine machines available. They eventually received more modern equipment from their allies, such as Spads and Sopwith Camels but they were in small numbers. By March 1918 the *AMB* had increased to twelve *escadrilles* of which one was a maintenance unit and another operated seaplanes. One of the *escadrilles*, though, still had Farmans, which had been condemned as operationally obsolete by the British in 1915.

One complication for those personnel operating from the airfield at Houthem was that squeezed into the same tiny village were the Belgian royal family, and the headquarters of the Belgian army. So every move was made under the gaze of the highest echelons of the powers-that-be.

A further by-product of the *AMB*'s small size was that it often fought alongside units belonging to its Allies, most commonly squadrons of the RNAS. But this in itself could be a mixed blessing as 4 Naval, perhaps the most active unit in Flanders, on more than one occasion attacked Belgian aircraft and forced them down. Fortunately, no Belgian fighter pilots were seriously wounded during these encounters.

Though small the *AMB* was an efficient and effective force and produced a number of aces, including Willy Coppens, who was the highest scoring kite balloon ace of any nation. Their skill flying obsolescent machines is demonstrated by the fact that all their aces survived the war.

Following the end of the 'Race to the Sea' towards the end of 1914, the front line remained in virtually the same place in the few miles near the coast until the final advance to victory in 1918. As a result the squadrons of the *AMB* tended to remain at the same airfields through the course of the war, not being moved about by the ebb and flow of the war. It was only during the 'last hundred days' that it was able to help in the final advance of the Allies, commanded in Belgium by King Albert who had been so instrumental in encouraging its formation just a few years before.

German ranks and their British equivalent

German army

German	British
Oberst	Colonel
Rittmeister	Cavalry Captain
Hauptmann	Army Captain
Oberleutnant	Lieutenant
Leutnant	Second Lieutenant
Fähnrich	Officer Cadet
Offizierstellvertreter	Warrant Officer
Feldwebel	Sergeant Major
Vizefeldwebel	No British equivalent
Unteroffizier	Corporal
Gefreiter	Private (First Class)
Flieger	Enlisted man
Pionier	Bavarian rank for *Flieger*

German navy

German	British
Kapitän	Captain
Kapitänleutnant	Lieutenant Commander
Oberleutnant zur See	Lieutenant
Leutnant zur See	Sub Lieutenant
Oberflugmeister	Chief Petty Officer
Flugmeister	Petty Officer

Abbreviations

AEO	Assistant Equipment Officer
AFC	Air Force Cross
AFC	Australian Flying Corps
BE	Bleriot Experimental
CB	Companion of the Bath
CBE	Commander of the Order of the British Empire
CMG	Companion of the Order of St Michael and St George
CO	Commanding Officer
CVO	Commander of the Royal Victorian Order
CWGC	Commonwealth War Graves Commission
DCM	Distinguished Conduct Medal
DFC	Distinguished Flying Cross
DFM	Distinguished Flying Medal
DH	De Havilland
DSC	Distinguished Service Cross
DSO	Distinguished Service Order
EA	Enemy aircraft
FA	*Flieger Abteilung*
FA(A)	*Flieger Abteilung(A)*
FE	Farman Experimental
FEA	*Flieger Ersatz Abteilung*
FB	Fighting Biplane
GC	Group Captain
GCB	Knight Grand Cross of the Bath
GCMG	Knight Grand Cross of the Order of St Michael and St George
HA	Hostile aircraft
JG	*Jagdgeschwader*
KB	Kite Balloon
KBE	Knight Commander of the Order of the British Empire
KCB	Knight Commander of the Order of the Bath
KG	Knight of the Order of the Garter
LVG	*Luft-Verkehrs-Gesellschaft*
MC	Military Cross
NCO	Non Commissioned Officer
OC	Officer Commanding
OM	Order of Merit
POW	Prisoner of War
RAF	Royal Air Force
RAS	Reserve Aeroplane Squadron
RE	Reconnaissance Experimental
RFC	Royal Flying Corps
RN	Royal Navy
RNAS	Royal Naval Air Service
SE	Scouting Experimental
USAS	United States Air Service
VAD	Voluntary Aid Detachment
VC	Victoria Cross

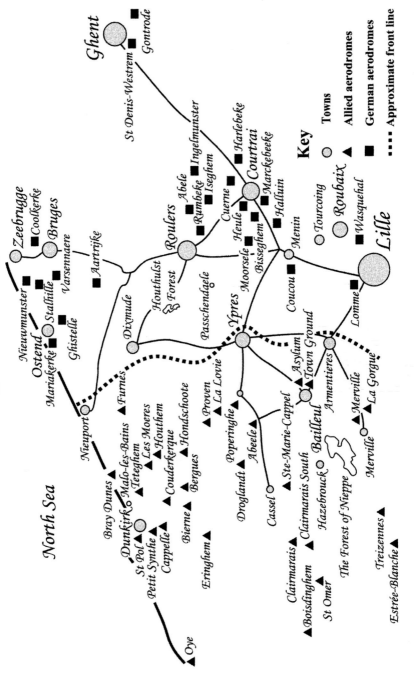

'The Channel Coast

The Eastern Area

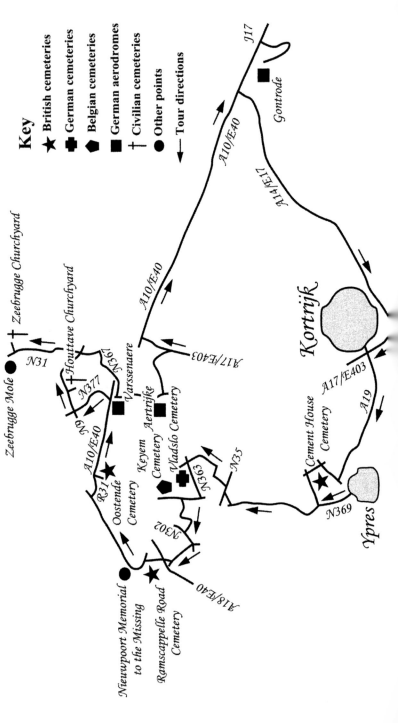

Key

★ British cemeteries
✚ German cemeteries
⬟ Belgian cemeteries
■ German aerodromes
† Civilian cemeteries
● Other points
→ Tour directions

Zeebrugge Mole
Zeebrugge Churchyard
N31
Houttave Churchyard
N377
N367
Varssenaere
A10/E40
N9
R31
Oostende Cemetery
Keyem Cemetery
Aertrijke Cemetery
Vladslo Cemetery
N363
N35
A10/E40
A17/E403
Nieuwpoort Memorial to the Missing
Ramscappelle Road Cemetery
N302
A18/E40
Cement House Cemetery
N369
A17/E403
A19
Kortrijk
Ypres
A10/E40
A14/E17
Gontrode
J17

Chapter One

THE EASTERN AREA

Leave Ypres on the N369 to Diksmuide, and approaching Diksmuide turn right N35 Esen. At the next roundabout, turn right N35 Roeselare. In front of the church in Esen, turn left for Vladslo. Continue north through the village, cross the N363 and follow the signs to the cemetery on the left hand side of the road.

Vladslo German Cemetery

The avid reader of the *Airfields and Airmen* series will know that this cemetery was covered in the *Ypres* volume page 146. Since the publication of that book much more information has come to light and this spot will be the only one that will be visited for a second time.

For the Allies the Commonwealth War Graves Commission cemetery at Longuenesse (page 166) has the distinction of containing the largest number of British and Empire air service personnel from the Great War. For the Germans this honour is held by Vladslo, where there are about 250 air service casualties, both army and navy.

There are three casualties from the Jabbeke raid (page 57) and they are *Flugzeugmeister* Wilhelm Drews (2/1713), *Flugzeugmechanik* Friedrich Schramm (2/1635) and *Flugzeugmatrose* Wilhelm Grabowski (2/1626).

The first graves we are visiting are those of Hermann Kirchner (5/1291), Karl Mahr (5/1272), Gustav Ruske (5/1289) and Otto

Schwarz (5/1287). They died when their airship, the *LZ37*, was shot down by Rex Warneford, for which he received what was only the second Victoria Cross awarded to an airman. They are situated in the middle of Plot 5, which is in the far right corner.

Rex Warneford VC

Reginald Alexander John Warneford was born at Darjeeling on 15 October 1891, the son of an engineer on the Indian railways. He was brought to England as a small boy but when the family returned to India he continued his education at the English College, Simla. Apprenticed to the merchant marine, he joined the India Steam Navigation Company and was in Canada awaiting a return to India when war was declared. Warneford sailed for Britain and joined the army but almost straight away transferred to the RNAS for pilot training.

Flight Sub-Lieutenant Rex Warneford VC.

Initial tuition was carried out at Hendon and after further tutelage at Upavon he gained his Royal Aero Club certificate, No. 1098, on 25 February 1915. The Commander of Naval Air Stations was Commander R M Groves, known as 'The Crasher' due to the unfortunate frequency with which he smashed aeroplanes. One of his subordinates was Warren Merriam, a noted pre-war flier, who was Warneford's flying instructor. In his book *First through the Clouds* Merriam wrote:

> Commander Groves was a sportsman all the way, and, as I found in the case of Warneford, who gained the V.C. for destroying a Zeppelin, he had a keen eye for a good pilot. Had it not been for Groves, I am certain that Warneford would never have had the chance to display his valour.
>
> Warneford was then a probationary officer pupil at Hendon. Squadron Commander Sitwell, a pukka navy man who was drilled in its strict school of discipline, took the view that Warneford would never make an officer from the disciplinarian point of view, and he was about to send a report to headquarters

to that effect. I had insisted that I was more than satisfied with his flying. Warneford was, in fact, a born aviator. He had mastered the intricacies of flight with amazing swiftness, and, as he was completely without fear, my only difficulty was to check his over-confidence. I knew that only a special effort would get Warneford through, so, during a chance visit by Commander Groves, I seized the opportunity to ask Warneford to make the best show he could before him. The Commander was so impressed by Warneford's brilliant flying that he made the remark: 'This youngster will either do big things or kill himself'. It is sad indeed that, when the time came, he could not do one without the other.

Warneford was posted to 2 Wing on the Isle of Sheppey, where it was recognised that he was an individual who disliked mundane discipline and it was arranged that he be posted to an operational unit. Thus on 7 May 1915 Warneford was posted to 1 Wing at Furnes (page 123) on the Belgian coast. Over the next few weeks he demonstrated his aggressiveness with attacks on German troops and guns, as well as any German aeroplanes he met. He was allocated his own machine, a Morane-Saulnier monoplane, and was given a roving commission by his commanding officer. On 17 May 1915 Warneford, together with his gunner, Leading Mechanic G E Meddis, encountered the airship *LZ39* setting out for a raid over Britain. Despite machine gunning it, the airship escaped by jettisoning ballast and climbing out of range.

In the late evening of 6 June 1915 a message was received from the Admiralty in London that three airships were returning from a raid on England. Four machines were ordered into the air. Two aeroplanes were directed to bomb the airship sheds at Evere near Brussels and the other

Morane-Saulnier Type L No.3253 in which Warneford brought down the *LZ*37.

The army airship *LZ*37. On the left can be seen the forward gondola in which Alfred Müller had his miraculous escape.

two to attempt an interception. Warneford took off in his Morane, without an observer, at 0100 hours on 7 June, equipped with six 20lb bombs. While near Dixmude he spotted an airship over Ostend and set off in pursuit. He finally caught up with the airship after forty-five minutes near Bruges and was met with defensive fire. Warneford turned away and gained height for an attack from above. For twenty minutes the airship and Warneford conducted a game of cat and mouse, with the *LZ*37 attempting to shoot him down while he endeavoured to get above it. Eventually Warneford reached a height of 11,000 feet and was able to glide down. Flying the length of the giant, commencing from the stern, he released his bombs. At first there was no effect but then an explosion ripped the front section apart. The airship disintegrated in a massive fire and fell to earth. It crashed on a convent killing two nuns, a man and a child, as well as injuring others. Amazingly one of the crew of nine survived to tell the tale. Alfred Müller, the airship's coxswain, wrote:

> *I rushed from the wheel to the gondola door; I was overcome by terror. What had happened? A crackling, rattling sound, otherwise there was dead silence in the gondola.*
>
> *The commanding officer was slumped over the side; the first officer lay over the chart table; the (others) had fallen to the floor of the gondola. Nobody moved. Were they unconscious? I just stood there. What had happened? A shudder of horror. A quick look at the rear gondola brought a new terror. Almighty God! The ship was on fire!*
>
> *I was heading straight for my death. 'I don't want to be burned alive!' a voice inside me cried. Thoughts rushed through*

28

The wreckage of *LZ*37 in the outskirts of Ghent.

The crew of *LZ*37. On the night they were shot down there were nine members. Alfred Müller is second from the left, back row.

my mind in a mad storm: my whole life, my wife, my parents, my brothers and sisters – I saw them all around me reading my obituary. Good God, the thoughts that crowded into the brain in those few seconds! Slowly I sank to the floor. Glowing, smouldering pieces of fabric from the ship's covering fell on my face and neck, and on my comrades. I felt another thunderous crashing and shuddering. The airship had broken up. I lost consciousness.

An impact brought me round again. I was still alive. Had I dreamed it all? Or had a miracle happened? How had I got here? Was I still falling?

No, I was on a bed, and a nun was standing by me. I stared at her wide-eyed. Above us were the flames crackling loudly, and a beam fell in. How could I escape? I ran as best as I could, this way and that – there was no way out! Was I to burn here, after surviving the very greatest danger? Where was that nun? Why did she leave me alone? Parts of the ceiling were caving in, bringing large sections of the wall with them.

There was a light coming through a gap! Was it a way out? No, the ship's skeleton lay just outside. I hurled myself against it with all my force, but sprang back. I tensed my muscles. In desperation I made a jump through the distorted half open door. The waist clasps of my leather coat caught on something, but the force of my leap tore them out. I landed outside amid the burning wreckage of the ship, and dashed through the glowing, smouldering remains.

As the wreckage had fallen, the forward gondola, containing Müller, detached and crashed through the convent roof, depositing him on a bed. The explosion of *LZ37* had thrown Warneford's machine upside down but, having regained control, he was forced to land many miles behind enemy lines as his engine had stopped. Inspecting the engine he found a disconnected fuel pipe and after 35 minutes of repair work he was able to restart his engine and take off. Unfortunately, due to fog he was unsure of his position and eventually landed on the beach at Cap Gris Nez. Once daylight came he was able to obtain more fuel from a nearby French unit and returned to Furnes at about 1030 hours.

This was the first time an aeroplane had brought down an enemy airship, and Warneford received a telegram from the Admiralty conveying the congratulations of King George V and notifying him of the award of the Victoria Cross. On 17 June Warneford received the *Legion d'Honneur* from General Joffre. Following a celebratory lunch,

The funeral of Rex Warneford at Brompton Cemetery.

Warneford travelled to the aerodrome at Buc near Paris to collect a new aeroplane for delivery to the RNAS at Furnes. He made one short test flight and then flew a second one carrying Henry Beach Newman, an American journalist, who had never flown before. During a climb to approximately 200 feet the right wings collapsed and the machine disintegrated. Warneford and Newman, who were not strapped in, were both flung out. Beach was killed instantly and Warneford died on his way to hospital. On 21 June Warneford was buried at Brompton Cemetery in London, with the ceremony being attended by thousands of mourners.

Sous-Lieutenant **Edmond Thieffry**

The next grave we are visiting contains *Flugobermatrose* Luitjen Luitjens (2/1372) and is in Plot 2, which is located towards the top left corner. His death is associated with one of the great Belgian aces, Edmond Thieffry.

The *Aviation Militaire Belge (AMB)* was particularly strict on the confirmation of aerial victories, much like the French. If the same system had been employed as the British the scores of the Belgian fighter pilots would be much higher. For instance if you examine the victory list of Andre de Meulemeester, the second most successful Belgian ace, you will see that in addition to his eleven confirmed victories, he had another nineteen unconfirmed claims!

Luitjens was born on 16 March 1891 at Eckel. He joined *MFJI*, commanded by *Leutnant zur See* Gotthard Sachsenberg (pages 60 and 65),

31

Luitjen Luitjens in front of his Albatros.

on 3 June 1917 at Aertrycke. When he was shot down and killed on 22 August 1917 he had not claimed any victories. He almost certainly was the eighth victory of Thieffry.

Edmond Thieffry was born at Etterbeck near Brussels on 28 September 1892. Shortly before the war began he qualified as a lawyer. Taken prisoner in the very early part of the war he managed to escape via neutral Holland on a motorbike. After learning to fly at Étampes in the summer of 1915, he was posted to the *5me Escadrille* at Houthem (page 86). On 15 March 1917, while flying a Nieuport Scout, he achieved his first official victory when he destroyed a German two-

Edmond Thieffry and his Nieuport Scout. The comet on the fuselage was the insignia of the *5me Escadrille*. He was the unit's only ace.

seater. On 3 July he became the first Belgian to claim two victories in a day. As a result of this feat he was commissioned and made a *Chevalier de l'Ordre Leopold* and was awarded the *Croix de Guerre*. The boot was firmly on the other foot on 31 August when he was shot down himself, landing just inside the Belgian front line, though he was unscathed.

After Luitjens, Thieffry claimed two more enemy machines, the last being on 9 November 1917. In addition to his ten confirmed claims, making him the third most successful Belgian fighter pilot of the Great War, he had another five unconfirmed victories. Most of these were claimed while flying the Nieuport, though the latter ones were gained while flying the Spad.

His luck finally ran out on 23 February 1918 whilst attacking a two-seater, when his Spad was shot down by the observer behind the German lines. He had flown 160 patrols and been involved in fifty-three combats. Admitted to Ghent Hospital, it was some weeks before the Belgian authorities knew he was alive. In April 1918 he escaped from the prisoner of war camp at Karlsruhe but was recaptured ten days later.

Wreckage of Luitjens' Albatros.

After the end of the war, he arrived home in Brussels on 6 December 1918. He resumed his legal activities and entered local politics, while still maintaining a great interest in aviation. He flew on the first Sabena flight to the Belgian Congo in February 1925 and remained there participating in other flights. On 11 April 1929 the aeroplane in which he was flying was caught in a tropical storm and crashed, killing him. For his activities in the Congo he was made an *Officier de l'Ordre Leopold I*.

Marinefeldjagdstaffel **Neumunster in front of a Fokker** *Eindecker.* **Josef Wirtz is seated on the extreme right.**

An aerial collision

The next grave (2/1910) at which we are paying our respects is another German naval flyer, *Vizeflugmeister* Josef Wirtz, and is situated in the same Plot as Luitjens.

Wirtz was born on 3 March 1898 at Oldenkirchen and joined *MFJI* in November 1916. His first victory, on 7 February 1917, was a Sopwith 1½ Strutter of 5 Wing RNAS. The crew, Flight Lieutenant C R Blagrove and Air Mechanic Second Class J Milne, were killed and are buried at Ghent.

On 24 April a formation of seven FE2s of 20 Squadron left on an escort to a reconnaissance by the Sopwith 1½ Strutters of 45 Squadron. Just east of Ypres twelve Albatros scouts were spotted and attacked. In the ensuing battle three FE2s were brought down, one in the enemy lines and the other two just on the Allied side. However five machines were claimed by German pilots, Werner Junck and Walter Göttsch of *Jasta* 8 (pages 39 and 126), Walter von Bülow of *Jasta* 18 and two by Josef Wirtz of *MFJI*.

It would appear that Bülow claimed the machine flown by Second Lieutenant N L Robertson and his observer Captain R M Knowles MC.

Major James Abbey of the RFA sent this report to the officer commanding 20 Squadron:

I beg to report that an aeroplane, No. 5144, belonging to your Squadron, landed in flames on my battery position about 8 a.m. this morning and was totally destroyed.

The machine burst into flames at a great height and was landed safely in our lines owing to the gallant conduct and great presence of mind of the two occupants, the Pilot Lt Robertson R.F.C., and Observer Capt. Knowles, R.F.C.

Though both these officers were wounded, the Pilot rather seriously in two places, and both were burnt slightly, they managed to keep the flames under control until within 200 feet of the ground, Knowles then jumped clear just before the machine turned over, and pulled Robertson from under the burning wreckage.

Capt. Knowles was full of praise at the manner in which Lt. Robertson piloted him safely to ground.

The action was not one sided though, as 20 Squadron shot down one Albatros in flames and sent another out of control. *Leutnant* Fritz Kleindienst of *Jasta* 18 was killed in this area and at about this time. The commanding officer of the unit, Karl von Grieffenhagen, was also seriously wounded in action during the day, so both may have been victims of 20 Squadron.

From evidence on the German side it would seem that Wirtz received credit for one FE but the second one was awarded to him after he had collided with it and been killed. The crew of the second FE2 were H R Nicholson and A R Johnston.

The wreckage of Wirtz's Albatros DIII.

The wreckage of FE2d No.A6385 in which Nicholson and Johnston were killed.

Harry Reid Nicholson

A Canadian from Hamilton, Ontario, Nicholson served in the Canadian Pioneers before joining the RFC in early 1917. He attended the School of Military Aeronautics at Reading and was posted overseas on 18 March 1917. He had only served with 20 Squadron a month before he was killed and has no known grave.

Alfred Roy Johnston

Born on 17 May 1895, he came from Bedford. Joining the RFC in early 1916, he also trained at Reading. After further training at No. 9 Reserve Squadron he joined 20 Squadron. On 1 March 1917 he was promoted to flight commander. Like his observer he also has no known grave and is commemorated on the Arras Memorial to the Missing.

Return to the N363 and turn right at Dixmuide. Continue through Beerst, turn right for Oostende (N369). Entering Keiem, turn right into the village at the *Belgish Militair Kesthof* sign. Follow the signs through the village to the cemetery on the right.

Keyem Belgian Cemetery

This cemetery has a very distinctive diamond shape and contains 628 graves. The cemetery sign still shows Keyem though the modern spelling is Keiem. As you enter on the left hand side are several rows of headstones. In the front row at the left hand end is the grave of J A A Pauli (see also page 65). In the cemetery register he is Jan but his headstone shows Jean.

Jan Adolf Amaat Pauli (450)

He was born on 24 August 1891 in Lille, France. Having gained his brevet, *Sergent* Pauli was posted to the *3me Escadrille*, led by *Commandant* R Dhanis, on 5 April 1917. His first operation was flown four days later, but he was not involved in a combat until 24 April, when attacked while engaged on artillery cooperation. The unit was flying the obsolete Farman F40 pusher aeroplane, a type of machine the British had ceased using on the Western Front two years earlier, in 1915.

Jan Pauli.

Just a week later, while flying an F40 on another artillery sortie, Pauli and his observer, Lieutenant Jean de Bersaques, were attacked by six enemy scouts over Dixmude. Though the escort of *Adjutant* Jacques Goethals engaged two of them, the others brought down the F40 in flames. Pauli had only flown seven operations and the combination of an obsolete machine and inexperienced pilot proved fatal. They were shot down either as the first victory of Gotthard Sachsenberg of *MFJI* (pages 60 and 65) or the twenty-fourth claimed by Karl Emil Schäfer of *Jasta* 28 (*Ypres* pages 105 and 126).

Pauli's remains were re-interred at Keiem on 6 November 1920. He was posthumously awarded *l'Ordre de Léopold* and the *Croix de Guerre*, as were all Belgian fatal casualties.

Armand J F Glibert (494)

On the extreme right of the burial ground in the back row is the grave of Armand Glibert. He was shot down and killed on 8 April 1917 as the eighth victory of the *Jasta* 8 ace, Walter Göttsch.

Glibert was born on 16 January 1889 at Etterbeek, Brussels and served with the *12me Regiment de Ligne* before joining the *AMB*. After pilot training he was posted to the *6me Escadrille* based at Houthem, commanded by *Capitaine* Hédo, who were flying two-seater machines. His first flight with them was on 31 March 1916. Almost a year later on 8 April 1917, on his fortieth operational flight, he and his observer, Jules Callant, were detailed for a long reconnaissance to Bruges. Despite the fact that Glibert had been in the unit for a year this was to be his first combat. They were attacked by three Halberstadt scouts and shot down, then were later found in their demolished BE at Couckelaere.

Armand Glibert.

This was the only Belgian BE2 lost to enemy action. In order to improve the performance of their BE2s the Belgians had replaced the 90hp RAF engine with a 150hp Hispano-Suiza and then swopped the positions of the occupants, such that the observer was now at the rear and had a ring-mounted Lewis gun. The pilot who was now in the front, had a fixed forward-firing Vickers machine gun. Unfortunately, the extra weight meant that the service ceiling was now only about 11,000 feet. These modifications had been officially supervised by Glibert and his inability to climb may have contributed to his loss.

Callant's body was disinterred in August 1921 and buried in Charleroi.

The BE2 in which Armand Glibert and Callant were killed.

Walter Göttsch in his Fokker Triplane.

Walter Göttsch

The reader may remember that Göttsch was the pilot of an Albatros which shot down an FE2 of 20 Squadron on 7 January 1917 as a result of which the pilot, Sergeant Thomas Mottershead, earned the Victoria Cross (*Ypres* page 62). He was also credited with a DH2 of 29 Squadron on 17 November 1916, when Captain S E Cowan and Second Lieutenant W S F Saundby were killed (*Cambrai* page 172).

Born on 10 June 1896 near Hamburg, Göttsch saw action with *FA*33 in Flanders during 1916. On 10 September 1916 he was posted to *Jasta* 8, based at Rumbeke, as a *vizefeldwebel*. The unit was formed on this date utilising personnel from *FA*6, *FA(A)* 213, *FA*40 and *FA*33. Its first victory was claimed on 1 October by *Vizefeldwebel* Alfred Ulmer (page 126).

Göttsch claimed his first victory on 14 November 1916, a Belgian kite balloon whose observers survived. On 3 February 1917, having shot down six Allied machines, he was wounded in a fight with an FE2 of 20 Squadron, crewed by Second Lieutenant C Gordon Taylor and Captain R M Knowles. The latter also figures in another incident on page 34. No. 20 Squadron played an important part in Göttsch's career, as he shot down seven of their machines. In addition he was shot about by one of their aircraft on 29 June and wounded again in an encounter with them on 25 September 1917. Following his twelfth victory he was awarded the Knight's Cross with Swords of the Royal Hohenzollern House Order. On 16 September he scored his seventeenth victory, which made him *Jasta* 8's most successful pilot of the war. He was posted to *Jasta* 19 on 14 February 1918 as commanding officer.

With this unit he claimed three more victories, the last being an RE8 of 52 Squadron on 10 April 1918. The machine, crewed by Second Lieutenant H Lumsden Taylor and his observer, Lieutenant W I E Lane, was able to make a forced landing on the Allied side of the lines, though both occupants were wounded. However, Lane had fired a well-placed burst at the attacking Fokker Triplane and shot it down in flames. They landed close to the burning remains of the enemy machine, which was allocated the captured enemy machine number G163.

Göttsch had been killed while claiming his twentieth victim, which at the time was considered the minimum requirement for the *Pour le Mérite* or 'Blue Max'. This could not be awarded posthumously and thus he did not receive it. In 1920

Henry Lumsden Taylor.

Lumsden Taylor received a request, via the Air Ministry, for information concerning the position of the crash site from Göttsch's friends in Germany.

Return towards the centre of the village and turn right to Stuivekenskerke and Pervijze. In Pervijze turn right N355 Nieuwpoort. Continue north, and turn right Ramskapelle N356. Continue through the village to the T-junction by the motorway. Turn right at Andere Richtigen and continue to the next T-junction where you will see the cemetery on the corner on the left side of the road. Turn left onto the main road (N367) and park.

Ramscappelle Road Military Cemetery

This area was occupied by XV Corps from June until November 1917, when they were holding the line from Sint Joris to the sea. As with a lot of other cemeteries it was greatly enlarged after the Armistice with casualties from other graveyards and isolated battlefield graves. There are now a total of 841 graves, of which over a third, 312, are sadly unidentified. There is no CWGC number for this cemetery as it was omitted from the over-printed yellow Michelin maps and was missed when producing the new handbook. However the War Graves Commission is aware of this and it will be included when the booklet is re-printed.

The last time I was here the headstones were badly worn. The first grave (VI E29) we are visiting is in the back row on the left and is twelve from the right. This is another highly decorated naval ace.

Harold Thomas Mellings (VI E29)

Mellings was born at Bromfield near Ludlow, Shropshire on 5 August 1897. He learned to fly at the Beatty School at Hendon and received his Royal Aeronautical Society certificate, or 'ticket' on 11 November 1915, flying a Caudron biplane. He joined the RNAS in April 1916 and after training was posted to 2 Wing in the Aegean. In this theatre of operations the navy was responsible for anti-submarine patrols, safe-guarding Allied ships and also supporting ground forces in Salonika.

Mellings arrived in the autumn of 1916 having travelled overland and then via Malta. During the next year he claimed at least four enemy machines destroyed flying 2 Wing's only Sopwith Triplane. In addition he was mentioned by Vice-Admiral Eastern Mediterranean Station for twice attacking submarines single-handedly and much other valuable service. He soon received the DSC and the Greek War Cross. In December 1917 Mellings received a Bar to his DSC before returning home on leave and in January 1918 he joined 10 Naval (later 210 Squadron RAF) at Teteghem, southeast of Dunkirk.

H T Mellings wearing the ribbon of his DSC and rosette for the Bar.

Melling's medals as displayed by his family today, including his death plaque in the centre.

The scroll that accompanied Melling's death plaque.

C Flight, 210 Squadron at Ste-Marie-Cappel. The nearest Camel, F5914 'S', was the machine in which Mellings was lost.

Gv RI

HE whom this scroll commemorates was numbered among those who, at the call of King and Country, left all that was dear to them, endured hardness, faced danger, and finally passed out of the sight of men by the path of duty and self-sacrifice, giving up their own lives that others might live in freedom. Let those who come after see to it that his name be not forgotten.

Capt. Harold Thomas Mellings
210th Sqdn. Royal Air Force

While with them he claimed another six victories but on 15 April was wounded by ground fire and transferred to 39 Stationary Hospital and then Whitechapel Hospital, London, where he was treated for a gunshot wound to the left thigh.

After convalescence he returned to 210 Squadron, claiming four more enemy machines shot down. On 22 July 1918 he led a six-man Offensive Patrol in the Dixmude – Bruges – Ostend area. One of his pilots was Kenneth Unger, featured in *Arras* page 78. It had been a busy day, Mellings had already claimed two victims on an earlier patrol, and the squadron had moved aerodromes from Teteghem to Eringhem, 35 kilometres south of Dunkirk. The patrol engaged various enemy groups and Mellings was last seen attacking a lower formation down at 200 feet, five miles south of Ostend.

Shortly before Melling's patrol returned another formation, led by Captains E D Crundall and H A Patey, took off on a sortie. They lost Lieutenant E H Bullen USAS, who was also killed. It would seem that both Mellings and Bullen fell foul of *Leutnant* Ludwig Beckmann of *Jasta* 56.

Melling's grave was found in Praatbosch Cemetery, near Vladslo, but was later moved to Ramscappelle Road. Bullen was a member of the United States Air Service and it would seem likely that his remains were repatriated home.

Ludwig Beckmann

Beckmann was known as 'Lutz' and came from Westphalia. He was posted to *Jasta* 6 in December 1917 and then to *Jasta* 48 in February 1918, but did not score in either unit. On 11 March he joined *Jasta* 56 and by August had claimed a total of eight victories and been given command of the unit. His last claim was on 5 September and was

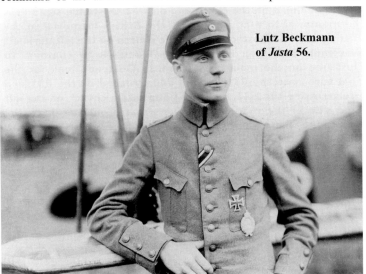

Lutz Beckmann of *Jasta* 56.

probably H A Patey of 210 Squadron. Another of his victims was probably M K Spidle of 17th Aero USAS (*Ypres* page 153).

In the Second World War Beckmann flew transport aircraft and commanded *Kgr zbV* 500 being awarded the Knight's Cross of the Iron Cross. He passed away on 20 January 1965 in Germany.

W P Bartlam (VI D2) and W Cosier (VI D3)

The next two graves we are visiting are in the row in front of Mellings and slightly to the right. They were involved in a strange incident which remains unsolved.

William Cosier, born in 1897, enlisted as an air mechanic third class on 19 January 1918. In civilian life he had been a textile drawer. Quite short, only just being over five feet tall, he came from Birmingham. On 27 September 1918 he joined the British Expeditionary Force and the following day was posted to 5 Group. At the beginning of the month he had re-mustered as a labourer, having been a wireless operator under training. On 12 October he was admitted to hospital but returned to duty shortly after.

Walter Percy Bartlam also came from Birmingham and was very young, being born on 5 June 1900. Enlisting on 29 May 1918, he had been a clerk in civilian life. Crossing the Channel on the same day as Cosier, he also was posted to 5 Group on 27 September. Like Cosier he had re-mustered from trainee wireless operator to labourer at the beginning of September.

Both of them were serving with 5 Group Works Section when, on 25 October 1918, they were shot and killed by assailants unknown, just two weeks before the Armistice.

Continue ahead on the N367, and pick up Oostende signs. Pass the memorial to King Albert and the British Memorial to the Missing towards Oostende. After the church on the left, turn left Westende Bad, then right at the T-junction to continue to Oostende on the main coast road. In Oostende look for the right turn onto the R31, Brussel E40. Proceed on the R31, and after crossing the N33, turn right opposite a church on the left hand side of the road, into Stuiverstraat. Continue down the street, and the cemetery will come into view on the right, behind a high brick wall. Parking is available outside the main entrance.

Oostende New Communal Cemetery

In October 1914, for a few days, Ostend was the seat of the Belgian government but on the 14th of the month the port was closed and the following day German forces occupied it. Allied troops re-occupied it on 17 October 1918. During the Second World War casualties from the evacuation of Belgium and France were buried here and during the war many flying casualties were also brought to this spot. There are now 50 burials from the Great War and a further 366 from the Second World War. The grave we have come to pay our respects to is second from the right in the rear row of the curved British plot on the right.

The first RNAS casualty (B28)

At the outbreak of war the RNAS's primary function was the protection of the BEF as it crossed to France. In order to maintain aerial reconnaissance a temporary seaplane base was established at Ostend. It was here that the RNAS suffered their first casualty.

Charles Edward Statham was born in Manchester, on 29 September 1885, the son of the late Samuel Edward and Jeanne Dorelee Statham. Before joining the navy he had been a machine fitter. He was quite short, measuring only five feet two inches. On his eighteenth birthday he enlisted for twelve years' service. He served in a number of ships and shore establishments and throughout this period his character was assessed as very good.

In July 1914 he was re-rated from able seaman to air mechanic. His war was to be very short as on 21 August 1914 he was accidentally shot in unknown circumstances at Ostend. Curiously, though he has a grave, he is also commemorated on the Memorial to the Missing at Nieuwpoort which you have just driven past.

Return to the R31 and turn right. Continue ahead to A10 Brussel, and join the motorway. Leave at Junction 6 Jabbeke and follow the signs for N377 De Haan over a number of roundabouts and junctions. Proceed north on the N377, then turn right at a roundabout for N9 Brugge. Turn right for Houtave (the sign for the turn off is half hidden behind advertising placards), and continue into the village to the church.

Houttave Churchyard

There is only one Commonwealth burial in this civilian cemetery, located at the right hand front of the church. On page 111 the loss of the first Sopwith Camel to enemy action is related but in fact the first fatal casualty in this type of machine on the Western Front occurred a month earlier, on 12 June 1917.

Langley Frank Willard Smith

Smith was born on 15 August 1897 in Philipsburg, Province of Quebec and was brought up by his grandmother, his father being a widower. His flying training began at the Thomas School in St Augustine, Florida, where he received near fatal head injuries when he accidentally stepped into a revolving propeller. His training finished with the Curtiss School in Newport News, Virginia and he received American certificate No. 521 on 29 June 1916. Arriving in England Smith completed further training at Chingford and Cranwell and received his Royal Aero club 'ticket', No. 3998, on 11 December 1916. He also gained a special Royal Aero certificate, No. 11, for a cross country flight from Chingford to **L F W Smith.** Eastchurch. During his tuition at Chingford he was graded as a *very good pilot indeed*.

Smith joined 4 Naval at Bray-Dunes on 17 April 1917 and flew his first operation on 28 April. Only two days later he claimed his first German machine, an Albatros scout, east of Nieuport. On 25 May he sent a Gotha shot down into the sea, though this was shared together with A J Chadwick, G H T Rouse and E W Busby. Smith brought down his last victory, his eighth, on 6 June, all of them while flying the Sopwith Pup.

Smith was an aggressive and confident pilot who flew his machines to the limit. Perhaps surviving the near fatal accident in Florida made him feel invincible. With the delivery of the first Camels to 4 Naval he was operating a much superior machine, more suited to his style of flying. On 13 June 1917 the Germans attacked London for the first time using their Gotha GIV machines (page 121). At 1100 hours a report was received that bombs were dropping on London, so seven machines from 4 Naval were sent up to intercept them, with Smith being one of the last to leave. He was not seen by the rest of the patrol during the flight. An enemy formation was driven back towards Bruges. At 1200 hours a dark coloured machine was sighted spinning down with a wing missing. It was believed that Smith's aeroplane had broken up. In only little more than five weeks of operational flying Smith was awarded the DSC, Belgian *Croix de Guerre* and *l'Ordre de la Couronne* and been Mentioned in Despatches.

Return to the N9 and turn right. On reaching the N31, turn left for Zeebrugge. In Zeebrugge, the sign for Zeebrugge Bad takes you through the underpass on the motorway, to a roundabout beyond. Follow the signs for P & O Ferries, and just before the Car Ferry Check In turn right into a car park and drive to the edge of the dock. You are now parked on the old Mole at Zeebrugge, and with suitable manoeuvring, the light at the end of the original pier should be in view to your left.

Zeebrugge Mole

The old mole has now largely disappeared as a new and larger sea defence has been built on the seaward side. This spot is of interest for two reasons. Firstly, it was an important base for German seaplanes operating in the North Sea and the great naval pilot and Blue Max holder, Friedrich Christiansen, was based here. Secondly, the famous raid by the Royal Navy to block the port of Bruges took place here on St George's Day, 23 April 1918.

Picture No.1. The Mole looking north in 2004.

Zeebrugge Mole

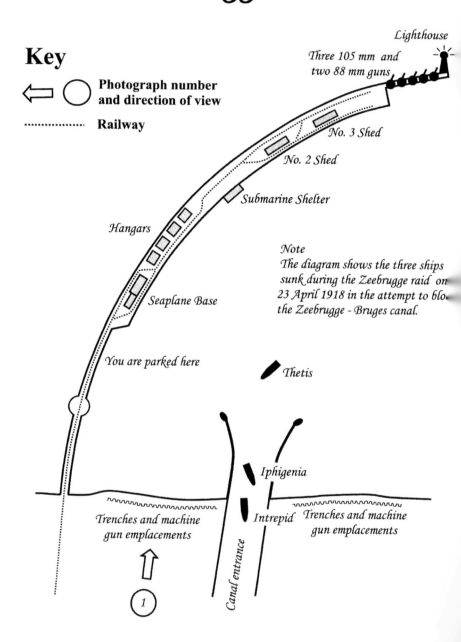

Key

⬅ ◯ **Photograph number and direction of view**

······· **Railway**

Lighthouse

Three 105 mm and two 88 mm guns

No. 3 Shed

No. 2 Shed

Submarine Shelter

Hangars

Note
The diagram shows the three ships sunk during the Zeebrugge raid on 23 April 1918 in the attempt to blo the Zeebrugge - Bruges canal.

Seaplane Base

You are parked here

Thetis

Iphigenia

Trenches and machine gun emplacements

Intrepid

Trenches and machine gun emplacements

Canal entrance

1

German seaplanes

After the occupation of the Belgian coast and its associated ports a seaplane station was established on the mole in December 1914. It became the largest and most active of the German navy seaplane bases in Flanders and there were at times up to fifty aircraft based here. The machines were kept fully assembled on specially constructed flat trucks in the railway station hall at the shore end of the mole. Also on the wagons were the necessary spares and stores for minor repairs, as well as fuel and oil. Locomotives were kept with steam up to pull the trucks out onto the mole, where cranes would lift the seaplanes off and lower them on to the calm water protected by the sea wall. Because of this, it was a rare event when the machines could not take off.

The machines based here were a thorn in the side of Royal Navy operations in the North Sea. They were responsible for the loss of a number of RNAS flying boats operating from the east coast which were conducting reconnaissance and anti U-boat operations. The biplane Brandenburg W12 and monoplane W29 seaplanes were formidable foes and the less manoeuvrable British flying boats were no match for them. The most successful of the German seaplane pilots was Friedrich Christiansen.

Oberleutnant zur See Friedrich Christiansen

Born on 12 December 1879 he was the son of a sea captain. He served in the merchant navy for some years and shortly before the war learned to fly and was awarded his aviator's certificate, No. 707. Called up as a naval aviator on the outbreak of war he was stationed at Zeebrugge from January 1915. In April 1916 he was awarded the Iron Cross First Class for his patrols over the North Sea, which included bombing Dover. On 27 April 1916 he received the Knight's Cross with Swords of the Royal Hohenzollern House Order. This was awarded for his general good work in scouting and bombing and not for the number of victories he had claimed, as was the case with the army's fighter pilots. In fact his first claim, a Sopwith Pup, did not occur until 15 May 1917. In September 1917 Christiansen was appointed commander of the Zeebrugge Naval Air Station.

On December 11 he, in company with two other Brandenburg W12 seaplanes, shot down the British

Friedrich Christiansen, commanding the station at Zeebrugge.

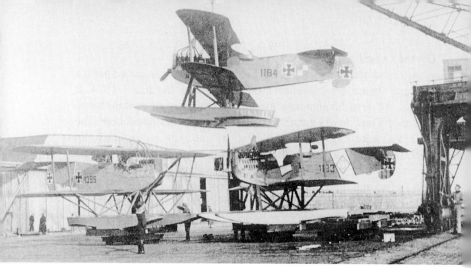

Christiansen's Brandenburg W29, with his markings of white floats and a letter C on the fuselage on the Zeebrugge Mole.

coastal airship C27, killing the crew of five, who have no known grave and are commemorated on the Chatham Naval Memorial. The same day he was awarded the *Pour le Mérite*, the first of only three given to naval aviators and the only one to a seaplane pilot. By this stage he had flown an amazing total of 440 operational flights. On 6 July 1918, he and four other W29 seaplanes attacked the surfaced British submarine C25 and killed six of the crew, including the captain. Though badly damaged and unable to submerge, it was able to make port. By the end of the war Christiansen had twenty-one official victories but whether this included the submarine and other surface vessels he had attacked is not clear.

After the war he flew the giant Dornier Do. X flying boat across the Atlantic then in 1933 joined the German Air Ministry. Recalled for duty on the outbreak of the Second World War he became commanding officer of occupied Holland. Imprisoned by the Allies at the end of the war, he was eventually released and died in West Germany on 5 December 1972.

The Zeebrugge Raid

The other great threat from Zeebrugge was U-boats. The port of Bruges, eight miles inland from the Belgian coast, provided a safe haven for up to 30 submarines. Exit to the North Sea was either down the ship canal to the harbour at Zeebrugge or via a series of minor canals, suitable for shallow draft vessels, to Ostende. Since 1914 a number of schemes had been proposed to bottle up the U-boats, ranging from blowing up lock gates to full scale landings. Unfortunately there were a number of obstacles to the various plans, including unknown German minefields, constantly changing sand banks and tide swept channels. In addition to these natural hazards the Germans had over 200 guns ranged along the coast, including several large calibre batteries.

When Haig's Flanders offensive, the Third Battle of Ypres, which was planned to occupy the Channel ports, ground to a halt in the autumn of 1917, after gaining only a few miles, the various plans were reviewed. It was decided to block the mouths of the two canals by employing a number of redundant light cruisers, while at the same time a force of marines would assault the Zeebrugge Mole and silence the guns arranged along it. In the early evening of 22 April 1918 the force set sail. The following day, St George's Day, despite heavy casualties, the ships were sunk in the mouth of the canal. The port of Bruges was denied to large draft vessels and the ships in port were unable to get out for three weeks, until the Germans removed part of two piers and dredged around the wrecks.

Much of the success of the operation relied upon the skill and inventiveness of one man, Wing Commander F A Brock RNAS, a remarkable and talented individual.

Frank Arthur Brock

Born on 29 June 1888, he was the son of Mr and Mrs Arthur Brock of Cheam, Surrey. He was the eldest of six brothers, all of whom attended Dulwich College, and was the only one to be killed during the First World War. On leaving school he joined and later became a director in his father's business, C T Brock and Company, the Crystal Palace Fireworks Limited of Sutton.

Shortly after the outbreak of war he obtained a commission in the Royal Artillery but a month later was lent to the RNAS for special work in connection with the Friederichshaven raid. During this daring operation, when the Zeppelin works on Lake Constance were attacked on 21 November 1914, one airship was damaged and the gas works hit.

F A Brock.

Brock was then transferred to the RNAS, being appointed a lieutenant RNVR on 31 December 1914 and founded the Royal Naval Experimental Station at Stratford in east London.

51

He received steady promotion and in April 1917 was made an acting wing commander. His inventiveness was put to good use and one of his most effective inventions was the Dover Flare, which was used to create an anti-submarine barrage across the Channel. He was also involved in the Brock Colour Filter. Perhaps his greatest contribution was the incendiary Brock ammunition, which was exceedingly effective against the hydrogen filled German airships. For this anti-Zeppelin work he received a special mention for valuable services. In January 1918 his OBE was gazetted for all the work he had done.

For the Zeebrugge raid the Dover Flare was unsuitable as it produced too much flame, so Brock and sixty ratings were lent to Admiral Keyes, commanding the operation. Brock was not only able to produce a much better flare but also a smoke float which produced smoke down on the surface of the sea, thus hiding the entire ship. Before this, smoke had been produced only from the funnels of warships. He also devised flares and other signalling devices for the operation.

During the initial part of the action Brock's smoke screen worked well, accompanied by an on-shore breeze which hid the attacking ships from the German guns. Unfortunately the capricious breeze later changed direction, nullifying the effect of the smokescreen. Brock had also devised two flame throwers which were mounted adjacent to the bridge of HMS *Vindictive*, the vessel that put the assault force ashore.

Fortunately at the end of the operation the smoke screen worked very well and enabled the force to withdraw with fewer casualties than might have been expected.

Brock went ashore on the mole, ostensibly to examine a range-finder that was mounted there and was never seen again. He is commemorated on the Chatham Memorial. Three of his RNAS party were also killed. Air Mechanic First Class Ernest Charles Poole is buried in Nottingham, Air Mechanic First Class Cedric A Wilkinson is buried in Adel, Yorkshire and Mechanic Second Class John Rouse has no known grave and is also commemorated on the Chatham Memorial.

Captain A F B Carpenter, captain of the *Vindictive*, who was awarded one of the eight Victoria Crosses for the Zeebrugge operation, said Brock had:

> *an extraordinary knowledge of almost any subject. He was no mean authority on old prints and books, was also a keen philatelist, was a great shot and all-round sportsman...*

One of Brock's Stratford party who participated in the raid, Sid Hesse, later emigrated to New Zealand and when he died on 20 November 2002 at the age of 102 was probably the last survivor of the Zeebrugge operation.

Return to the roundabout at the end of the motorway, and take the Zeebrugge Bad exit. At the traffic lights, turn left for Zeebrugge Centrum, and follow the Centrum signs over the metal bridge. Beyond the bridge, look for a church on the right hand side of the road. Turn right at the traffic lights by the church, and follow the road to park in front of the church.

Zeebrugge Churchyard

This is a most unusual cemetery and contains both German and Allied casualties. On the other side of the road there is the West Hinder lightship, which is now a tourist attraction. The large bed in front of the gate is a mass grave containing the crews of the German torpedo boats S15 and S20 killed on 5 June 1917. There are nine known, plus one unknown British aviators buried here.

Just inside the gate on the right is a memorial plaque to Wing Commander F A Brock, Lieutenant Commander A L Harrison VC, Lieutenant C E V Hawkins and Air Mechanic J Rouse, all missing after the Zeebrugge raid.

The first graves we have come to see are in the back row on the right and are next to each other.

Valentine Edgar Sieveking (169)
Both sides employed night bombers to create havoc behind each others' lines and 214 Squadron RAF (the old 14 Naval) were flying the enormous Handley Page 0/100 from Coudekerque (page 142) for this purpose. The threat from enemy night fighters was negligible, if not non-existent, but anti-aircraft fire was considerable and dangerous. For the story of the evolution of the Handley Page and history of 214 Squadron see *Ypres* page 178.

On the night of 18/19 May 1918 No. 214 Squadron lost a Handley Page to enemy anti-aircraft fire. The commander of the machine had had a very difficult start to his career. Born on 5 February 1892, Sieveking, whose parents lived in London, had been farming near St Leonards on Sea before joining the RNAS on 11 September 1915 as a probationary flight sub-lieutenant. Commencing flying training he was

Sieveking's Handley Page No. C3487 after its crash on the morning of 19 May 1918.

at Eastchurch in November 1915, where his personal report read:

> *Unlikely ever to become a pilot. Has paid no great attention to his work. This has been shown by test examination and two of his instructors have made request that they shall not continue to be sent up in a dual control machine with him. Has volunteered for observer work and I consider he might do well at it.*

Things got worse, as his report at Dover in February 1916 stated:

> *Not overburdened with intelligence. Rather slow and too heavy for observer.*

At Chingford in April 1916:

> *Is making no progress and is rather erratic and dangerous in the air and I do not consider his training as a pilot is worth continuing. I submit he may be discharged to shore and his flying has been suspended pending decision.*

However, Sieveking avoided this fate but in June crashed an RE7 at Cranwell, receiving abrasions on both legs, bruises on his face, a broken nose and suffering from shock. He hit two sheep on take off, one being thrown over the top plane and the other unfortunate animal being cut in half, before the aeroplane collided with a bank, wiping the undercarriage off. In November 1916 at Dover he turned a Nieuport over on landing and suffered shock.

By April 1917 Sieveking was serving with 7 Naval Squadron at Dunkirk, which had just started to receive Handley Page 0/100s, and was now adjudged to be *a zealous and hardworking officer*. The same month he attacked the seaplane base at Ostend, with his second bomb hitting a seaplane shed and setting it on fire. Returning to refuel and re-arm he then attacked Ostend seaplane base again. On 22 June his Distinguished Service Cross was gazetted. In July he bombed Varssenaere aerodrome and hit a dump, causing tremendous explosions and in October was appointed a flight commander. A Bar to his DSC was gazetted on 17 April 1918.

In May 1918, No. 214 Squadron, which had been formed in December 1917 from the old 7 Naval Squadron, was heavily engaged in attacking the docks and other targets in German occupied Belgium. The Handley Page load was generally three 550 lbs or fourteen 112 lbs bombs. Sieveking was airborne on four consecutive nights from 13 to 18 May. On the night of 18/19 May he had already completed one operation, when he departed from Coudekerque (page 142) on his second to bomb the Solway Works at Zeebrugge. Unfortunately, the anti-aircraft fire was deadly accurate and his machine was brought down. He and his observer, Henry Havilland-Roe, were killed but their gunner, Air Mechanic F Spencer, survived.

Henry Alfred Havilland-Roe (170)

Born on 1 August 1889, the son of Henry and Charlotte Julia Havilland-Roe, who came from Nottingham, Henry Alfred joined the RNAS at Eastchurch on 29 July 1917 and was gazetted a probationary flight sub-lieutenant the same day. He graduated as an observer officer on 5 January 1918 and arrived at Dunkirk four days later.

Hans von Rolshoven

On the opposite side of the cemetery from Sieveking's grave is a row of German headstones and the one we are interested in is in the middle.

The German navy had its own two-seater *Feldflieger Abteilungen* which, like their army counterparts, had single-seater Fokker *Eindeckers* attached to them. These ultimately developed into *Marine Feldjagdstaffeln* and by the end of the war there was a *Marine Jagdgeschwader* consisting of five *staffeln*.

Separate from the *marine abteilungen* and *marine jagdstaffeln* were the *seefrontstaffeln*. The first of these, *Seefrontstaffel I* (*SEE* I), was formed at the beginning of the war and was responsible for operating seaplanes over the North Sea. *Seefrontstaffel* II or *Marine Landstaffel Neumünster* II was established on 1 October 1917 and was equipped with Albatros DIIIs. Their task was to protect the seaplanes from marauding Allied fighter aircraft.

The first commander of *Seefrontstaffel* II was *Leutnant zur See* Hans von Rolshoven. He was born on 23 December 1894 in Straifund. Flying seaplanes from Zeebrugge with *SEE* I, he had been awarded the Iron

Hans von Rolshoven.

55

Rolshoven taxiing out for take off in Brandenburg W477 from the Zeebrugge Mole. He carried out a number of raids on England in this machine. In the background can be seen the entrance to the Zeebrugge to Bruges canal.

Cross First Class. On 2 October 1916 he was awarded the Knight's Cross with Swords of the Royal Hohenzollern House Order.

The first loss sustained by *SEE* II, which was based at Neumünster, just northwest of Bruges, was on 8 November 1917 when *Leutnant zur See* Ritter was shot down and killed west of Dunkirk. The first victory did not occur until 19 December 1917 when *Flugmeister* Albin Bühl shot down a DH4 of 5 Naval. The two crew members, Flight Sub-Lieutenant S S Richardson and Gunlayer R A Furby have no known graves and are commemorated on the Chatham Naval Memorial.

Rolshoven's funeral at Zeebrugge Churchyard.

Rolshoven claimed his first Allied machine on 7 September 1916, a Caudron, but there is no corresponding British, French or Belgian loss. His second, on 28 November 1917 was a DH5, possibly of 32 Squadron, who had a pilot wounded. His third and last was a Sopwith on 27 April 1918 but again there is no corresponding Allied loss.

On 6 May 1918 Rolshoven was killed in a flying accident at Zeebrugge in a Pfalz DIII. His successor was Reinhold Poss (page 119).

Retrace your steps over the metal bridge, and look for signs N31 Brugge. Follow these to rejoin the motorway, and continue south to Brugge. Turn right off the N31 onto the N367 Jabbeke. Continue ahead on the N367 until passing over the A10 motorway on a long right hand bend. After the end of the bend, take the second right turn into a small cobbled road, the Kasteldreef. Park in front of the concrete bollards leading to the pedestrian bridge over the motorway.

Jabbeke/Varssenaere Aerodrome

This aerodrome was known by the Germans as Jabbeke but to the Allies, particularly the RNAS, as Varssenaere. Occupied primarily by the flying units of the German navy, it was a frequent target for the RNAS and was photographed regularly. In August 1918, as part of the Allied offensive which eventually won the war, it was decided to deliver a knockout blow to the aerodrome. The plan was for some 50 Sopwith Camels from 210 and 213 Squadrons of the RAF, plus the 17th Aero USAS, to bomb from low level. In addition 204 Squadron was to patrol at 5,000 feet to prevent attack from above.

In his book *Fighter Pilot on the Western Front* Eric Crundall, a flight commander with 210 Squadron, described the raid:

All the Sopwith Camels in the squadron were each loaded with two high explosive and two incendiary bombs making four in all, which meant their maximum ceilings would be about 3,000 feet. Some considerable time before dawn the Camels took off three at a time in V formation. I was leading my Vee and made for the rendezvous position off Dunkerque where four squadrons of Camels would be in the two strings and an American squadron of Camels would escort us. In the dark it was very difficult to see the other formations and I did not spot

Varssenaere/Jabbeke Aerodrome

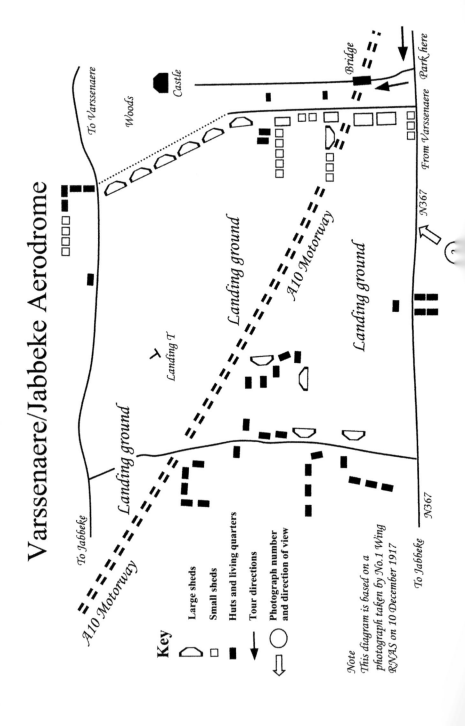

To Jabbeke

A10 Motorway

Landing ground

To Varssenaere

Woods

Castle

Landing T

Landing ground

A10 Motorway

Bridge

Landing ground

Park here

From Varssenaere

N367

N367

To Jabbeke

Key

◇ Large sheds

□ Small sheds

■ Huts and living quarters

→ Tour directions

○ Photograph number and direction of view

Note
This diagram is based on a photograph taken by No.1 Wing RNAS on 10 December 1917

anything until a Very Light was fired. By now it was not quite so dark and I managed to see the two strings of Camels and attached myself to the rear of the one on the right. My sight is not as good as it used to be and now long after the war I think I must have been suffering from eye strain due to lack of oxygen on very high flights. Several times lately in the daytime I have been surprised by enemy attacks when my pilots frequently spotted Huns before I did.

The arrival at Varssenaere was timed to take place at dawn so we flew along the coast at about 2,500 feet and two miles out to sea until we were opposite Zeebrugge. Then we turned to the right and started a shallow dive with full engine and passed over Zeebrugge at about 1,500 feet. We continued the shallow dive until we were near Varssenaere aerodrome at about 200 - 300 feet when one string of Camels passed over one side and the other string over the other side of the aerodrome.

It was beginning to get light when we arrived and we released our bombs on the hangars and buildings. Bombs were bursting when I dropped my four and my Camel was bumped about a bit but there was no shooting from the ground. There were fires and much smoke coming from the buildings on the aerodrome and we hedge-hopped our way along the surface until we crossed the

Picture No.2. Jabbeke looking northeast in 2004.

Sachsenberg's *nachfeier* or party to celebrate his *Pour le Mérite* on the night of 12/13 August 1918. Number 15 is Wilhelm Grabowski, killed in the raid the following morning. Number 13 is Osterkamp and number 10 is Sachsenberg.

lines. Every Camel returned safely to base and we were told later the Germans had been taken completely by surprise and the raid was a success.

Twelve Fokker DVIIs were caught in the process of starting engines and were machine-gunned, with 210 Squadron alone firing 9,200 rounds. At least eight of these were observed on fire. A fuel dump was set ablaze and other fires were started in hangars, sheds and living quarters. In 210's formation were H A Patey, I C Sanderson and Kenneth Unger (*Arras* page 78). No. 213's patrol included their commanding officer, Ronnie Graham.

Three German pilots and one ground crew member were killed during the attack, of whom three are buried in Vladslo (page 25). Three other personnel were wounded.

Later in the morning 211 Squadron flying DH9s dropped fourteen 112 lb bombs and one 230 lb bomb, starting more fires and confirming the damage from the earlier raid.

The previous evening there had been a party celebrating the award of the *Pour le Mérite* to *Leutnant* Theo Osterkamp, commanding *Marine Feldjagdstaffel* I and *Oberleutnant* Gotthard Sachsenberg, commanding the *Marine Jagdgeschwader*. They were the most successful marine pilots and their careers are covered in the Aertrycke aerodrome entry on page 63.

David Sinton Ingalls

One of the members of the 213 Squadron patrol which attacked Varssenaere was David Ingalls, who occupies a unique position, as he was the only United States Navy ace of the First World War.

He was born on 28 January 1899 in Cleveland, Ohio and his mother was a niece of US President William Howard Taft. Entering Yale University during 1916 he would eventually graduate with a BA in English in 1920. Enrolling in the First Yale Unit he became a member of the US Naval Reserve Flying Corps. Like Kenneth MacLeish (page 117) he learned to fly at West Palm Beach, Florida, and was then posted to New London, Connecticut, for submarine detection trials.

He eventually sailed for Europe on 23 September 1917 and after a short stay in London went on to Paris. Spending a couple of months awaiting orders, Ingalls was sent to the Gosport Flying School on 13 December, until February 1918. After a spell at Ayr in Scotland and in Paris, he arrived at the American Naval Station at St Pol near Dunkirk on 21 March 1918. As a result of the German spring offensive, the commanding officer of the unit offered his men and equipment to the British. Ingalls, MacLeish, Willis B Havilland and Kenneth R Smith were sent to 13 Naval at Bergues. But bad weather meant that Ingalls did not fly his first patrol until 6 April. After a number of patrols the Americans returned to Dunkirk. Following a short period with 218 Squadron RAF and other assorted tasks he was able, after a number of requests, to return to 13 Naval or 213 Squadron, as it had become.

Left to right: K R Smith, David Ingalls and Kenneth MacLeish (see page 117).

Camel D3422 of 210 Squadron was flown on the Varssenaere raid by Archie Buchanan. He was an American from New York and claimed four enemy machines in this aeroplane. On 30 October 1918 he was shot down and spent the last twelve days of the war as a prisoner.

His first patrol was on 9 August 1918 and only two days later he claimed an Albatros two-seater northeast of Dixmude, which he shared with another pilot. On 13 August he participated in the Varssenaere raid and wrote in a letter:

> *Certain parts of the aerodrome were assigned to each squadron as its target, and certain hangars or huts assigned to each man. The Huns were evidently asleep, and no Archie was put up until all the machines were down to about 200 feet, roaring over the country towards the objective, which was by this time plainly visible. The shrapnel bombs cause a ghastly looking explosion and the phosphorus give out clouds of smoke, so the field, upon looking back, seemed like a bit of Dante's Inferno.*
>
> *For several minutes all the machines were diving, zooming, turning and shooting from every side, resulting in a grand melée and many near collisions. Finally the leader fired a Very light, the signal to return. The countryside appeared to be covered with Camels streaking for the lines at about 100 feet up.*

During August and September Ingalls claimed a total of six victories, of which five were shared with other pilots. His last claim was on 23 September, a two-seater Rumpler which went down in flames, and he left 213 Squadron on 3 October. He spent the remainder of the war as a test pilot and instructor. After the war he qualified as a lawyer and during the Second World War served again in the US Navy, eventually retiring as a Rear Admiral USNR. He was also a vice-president of Pan American Airways and then president of the *Cincinnati Times-Star* newspaper. Ingalls died on 26 April 1985.

For his First World War service he was awarded an American DSC and a British DFC. The recommendation for the latter, written by Ronnie Graham, 213 Squadron's commanding officer, illustrates the regard he was held in:

> *His keenness, courage and utter disregard of danger are exceptional and are an example to all. He is one of the finest men this squadron ever had.*

Return to the main road, and turn right. Continue ahead, following signs for Jabbeke where available, until in Jabbeke turn left for Aartrijke. Continue into Aartrijke village, and turn right for Dixmuide. Leave the village downhill, round a long sweeping left hand bend then uphill again. Look for a pair of large brick pillars supporting ornamental gates on the left side of the road at the top of the slope. Turn left into the driveway immediately beyond the pillars. Drive to the turning area at the far end and park.

Aertrycke Aerodrome

This was essentially two aerodromes. In the north was Aertrycke and to the south Sparappelhoek, with the landing ground joining the two. *Marinefeldjagdstaffel* Nr. I was based here from 15 April to 10 September 1917. It is associated with the early careers of the two most successful German naval fighter pilots, Gotthard Sachsenberg and Theodor Osterkamp.

Picture No.3. The aerodrome looking northeast in 2005.

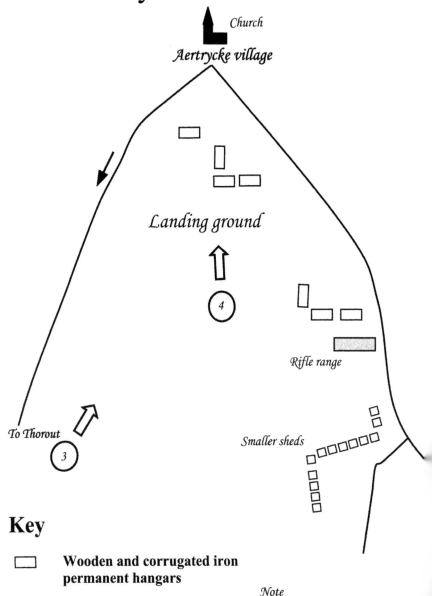

Aertrycke Aerodrome

Church

Aertrycke village

Landing ground

4

Rifle range

To Thorout

3

Smaller sheds

Key

Wooden and corrugated iron permanent hangars

Tour directions

Photograph number and direction of view

Note
This diagram is based on one draw[n] by No. 1 Wing RNAS on 27 Octo[ber] 1917

Gotthard Sachsenberg

Born on 6 December 1891 in Rossau, he became a sea cadet in 1913. After war was declared he flew as an observer with a naval flying unit. Awarded the Iron Cross First Class in 1915, he was commissioned as a *leutnant* early the next year. While instructing observers, Sachsenberg applied for pilot training and learned to fly at the *jastaschule* located near Mannheim. Rejoining his old unit *Marine FA2* in April 1916 he flew single-seater Fokker *Eindeckers*. In February 1917 he was made commander of *MFJ* I, despite not having scored a victory. His first victory, a Farman, occurred on 1 May 1917 and may have been *3me Escadrille's Sergent* Jean Pauli and Lieutenant Jean de Bersaques, though Karl Schäfer of *Jasta* 28 also claimed a Farman (page 37). On 20 August 1917, after achieving the relatively small total of six victories, Sachsenberg was awarded the Knight's Cross with Swords of the Hohenzollern House Order.

Sachsenberg scored at a steady rate and a year later, in August 1917 with approximately twenty-five victories, he was awarded the *Pour le Mérite*. As we have seen from the entry on page 57 the RAF livened up the celebratory proceedings with a heavy bombing raid! On 2 September 1918 he was made commander of *Marine Jagdgruppe* I, comprising the four Marine *jastas*. On 29 October he claimed his 31st and last victory. Following the end of the war he served with the *Marine Freikorps* in the Baltic. He died on 23 August 1961.

Picture No.4. *MFJ* I taking off at Aertrycke. The nearest machine, with diced marking on the fuselage is Sachsenberg. In the background can be seen the village church.

Sachsenberg (centre) and Osterkamp (right) at Kurland in 1919. On the left is the famous *Pour le Mérite* ace Josef Jacobs.

Theo Osterkamp

Born on 15 April 1892 at Duren, he was studying forestry when war was declared but then enlisted in the naval flying corps. Serving for the next two years as an observer with the marine flying units on the Belgian coast, he was commissioned in June 1916. Pilot training was completed in March 1917 and the following month Osterkamp joined *MFJ* I. In October he was made commander of *MFJ* II and remained so for the rest of the war. He claimed his first Allied machine only a day or so before Sachsenberg. Also, like his compatriot, he was awarded the Knight's Cross of the Hohenzollern House Order in August 1917 and then the coveted *Pour le Mérite* or 'Blue Max' a year later.

In September 1918 Osterkamp was flying a Fokker EV when he was shot down behind his own lines by three Spads but his life was saved by his parachute. By the Armistice he had claimed thirty-two victories, one more than his commanding officer, Sachsenberg. He also participated in the fighting in the Baltic in 1919 and 1920. In 1935 he joined the *Luftwaffe*, commanding *Jagdfliegerschule* I in 1939 and then *Jagdgeschwader* 51 at the beginning of the Second World War. In the early days of the conflict Osterkamp shot down six more Allied machines and on 22 August 1940 was awarded the Knight's Cross of the Iron Cross. He held various positions, rising to the rank of *leutnant-general*. He retired at the end of 1944, partly due to his criticism of the German high command. Held in high regard by his Second World War younger pilots, Osterkamp died at Baden-Baden on 2 January 1975.

Return to the village, and turn right to Brugge. Cross the N32 for E40 Ruddervoorde, and join the motorway northwards for E40 Brugge. At the motorway intersection follow E40 Gent. Continue eastwards on the E40 and leave at Junction 17 Wetteren. Turn right for Oosterzele (N42), and at the traffic lights turn right Centrum, then at the next lights right again into Geraadsberge. Proceed ahead on the N465 Melle, through the village of Gontrode. Just before the motorway underpass, turn left to Merelbeke. Look for a blue sign on right, showing two roads to the left. The first has No Entry signs, and the second is hidden behind the house beyond. Take this second left turn, continue up the road, and park by the concrete bunker. You are now in the centre of Gontrode aerodrome.

Gontrode Aerodrome

It was as a result of attacking the airship shed here on 22 April 1915 that Lanoe Hawker received the DSO. The hangar was damaged but not destroyed. He later received the first Victoria Cross for aerial combat (*Ypres* page 49 and *Somme* page 81).

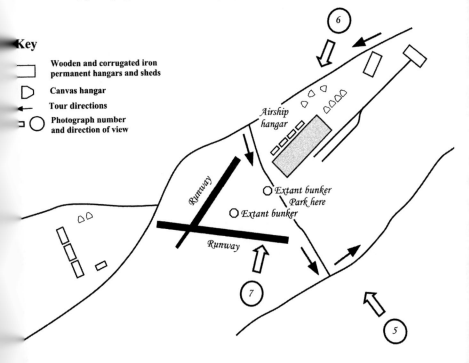

TURN LEFT HERE

BUNKER MARKS
POSITION OF
AIRSHIP HANGAR

AERODROME

Picture No.5. The aerodrome looking northwest in 2005.

Picture No.6. An oblique of Gontrode looking southwest during the First World War showing the airship shed.

The England *Geschwader*

With the Zeppelin having become largely ineffectual by early 1917, plans were made to bomb London using the new and large twin-engined Gotha bomber. This bombing campaign was given the code name *Turk's Cross*. In March 1917 *Kagohl* 1 was re-designated *Kagohl* 3, shortly after the first Gothas were delivered. The unit title derived from the fact they were a *Kampfgeschwader* or fighting squadron of the German Army High Command, *Oberste Heereesleitung* (*OHL*), hence *Kag* of the *ohl*.

Initially the unit consisted of four *staffeln*, each with six Gothas. *Staffeln* 15 and 16, plus the headquarters, were located at Gontrode, with *staffeln* 13 and 14 at St Denis-Westrem; both aerodromes were situated on the outskirts of Ghent. Because of range limitations the bombers would refuel at Neumünster, southwest of Zeebrugge.

The first two raids were in daylight on military targets in Kent and Essex but on 13 June 1917 the Gothas raided London for the first time. In almost unlimited visibility they dropped 4,400 kilogrammes of bombs, killing 162 people and injuring another 432. Unfortunately above all, from a propaganda point of view, one bomb landed on an infant's school in Poplar, east London, killing sixteen children and wounding thirty others. Surprisingly, given the weather conditions, not a single Gotha was shot down. Ernst Brandenburg, the commanding officer of the unit, became a national hero overnight. He was summoned to Supreme Headquarters the next day to receive his country's highest award, the *Pour le Mérite*, or Blue Max, from the Kaiser. A few days later returning to Ghent he was seriously injured in a take off crash. His replacement was Rudolf Kleine, an army officer of twelve years' experience, who had been a flight leader during 1915 in the old *Kagohl* 1. He was determined to maintain the assault on London and on 7 July 1917 a second raid was mounted in which 57 people were killed and 193 injured.

This second raid galvanized the politicians into action and Lloyd George appointed General Smuts, once a Boer rebel but now a senior officer in the British army, to chair a committee to review air organization and home defence. This raid, probably more than any other factor, influenced the recommendation by Smuts of a single, dedicated flying service which emerged on 1 April 1918 as the Royal Air Force, the world's first independent flying service.

Due to better British defences in the late summer and early autumn 1917 the Germans were forced to bomb England by night. In addition to the raids on England they were also attacking short-range targets behind the Allied front line – a task for which the large bombers were unsuited. It was during one of these missions that the Gotha carrying Rudolf Kleine was shot down and the crew killed (*Ypres* page 146).

Picture No.7. The Gothas of the England Squadron.

This was a psychological blow from which the squadron never really recovered.

The last attack on London by the England Squadron was on the night of 19/20 May 1918 when, out of an attacking force of twenty-eight Gothas, one landed in England and another five were shot down. In addition another crashed on the return flight. In fact more Gothas were lost in crashes than were shot down or missing, due to weather and the difficulty of operating large machines at night from small, ill-equipped aerodromes.

The squadron could not sustain losses like this, so attacks were restricted to short range targets, which continued until the Armistice but at significant cost to machines and crews. Though British civilian casualties were relatively low and the material damage of no great significance, the England Squadron had affected morale and their raids were a foretaste of the Blitz of the Second World War.

Continue across the airfield into a housing estate. Look for a left turn which will take you back across the airfield to the original entry point. Turn right, and retrace your steps back to Junction 17 on the E40 motorway. Join the E40 in the direction of Gent, and at the motorway intersection follow E17 Kortrijk. Proceed on the E17 until turning northwest on the E403 Brugge Ieper, then west on the A19 Ieper. At the end of the A19 turn right for Langemark on the N313. After Sint Juliaan turn left to Langemark (at Vancouver Crossroads). In Langemark turn left Bosinge and at the mini roundabout, turn left A19. The cemetery is ahead on the left side of the road.

Cement House Cemetery

This area was the scene of bitter fighting during the Third Battle of Ypres in the summer of 1917. It was in German hands throughout the war, apart from the period from August 1917 to April 1918 and September 1918 until the end of the war. It gets its name from a fortified farm building on the Langemark to Boesinghe road, which still remains as an ivy-covered bunker behind a farm. The original cemetery (No. 53) consists of what is now Plot I and contains 231 graves. It was used by a variety of units until April 1918. Plots II to XV were added post-Armistice as bodies were brought in from various cemeteries and the battlefield. About 500 French casualties were removed from Plots XVI, XVII and XVIII in 1922 and the space has been employed to bring in burials from other churchyards and communal sites where the maintenance of isolated graves could no longer be assured. The cemetery is used to bury remains that are still being found on the old battlefield. Sadly, of the 3,553 First World War casualties, a large proportion (2,385) are unidentified.

12 Squadron's first casualties (VIIA D9 and D8)

The two graves we have come to visit are located adjacent to the right and behind the Cross of Sacrifice. Plot VIIA is a small one, with only four rows, and our two casualties are in the second row near the right hand end.

In late 1915 R R Money, an observer in 12 Squadron, was detailed with a B Flight pilot to conduct a long reconnaissance over enemy lines to find enemy activity in Brussels. It was a cloudy day with a strong wind and, instead of finding themselves over Brussels, they arrived at Liège. Eventually navigating their way to the correct target they found little activity. Money continues the story in his book *Flying and Soldiering*:

> We turned back, and flew for nearly two hours before reaching the region of the War again, and, the cloud layer having dispersed, we felt frightfully exposed and naked while struggling along at about 35 miles an hour against the wind. We had stirred up a hornet's nest of Germans at Brussels, but luckily for us they were only a little faster than we were, and we started with the advantage of being at six thousand feet. Why they did not telephone the line aerodromes I do not know, but anyway we arrived home intact with only five minutes' petrol left. I had to go down to Headquarters with my report, and met with a very chilly

The original grave marker at Oostcamp Cemetery, comprising the rear fuselage of an aeroplane, most likely from Cunningham-Reid and Norman Gordon-Smith's machine.

reception. It was my first interview with Trenchard, and I understood why his nickname was Boom. He was expressing his disapproval of someone in no uncertain terms, and his voice did boom! – throughout the château! All he said to me was, 'H'm, you don't seem to have seen much,' but I came away cursing myself for a fool for not having given my imagination a certain amount of play. They sent another observer shortly afterwards, and although he stuffed his report fairly full, they still failed to express satisfaction. Then they sent Gordon-Smith and Cunningham-Reid, who never returned. (We heard afterwards that both were killed.) It was only the other day that I discovered, while reading a War diary of sorts, that a spy had reported that the Germans were making great preparations around Brussels, massing munitions and building encampments and a Zeppelin shed, in preparation for a great secret offensive against the Belgian Front. I was pleased to read these reports were never substantiated.

Gordon-Smith and Cunningham-Reid were our first fatal casualties, and we missed them very much. We had not yet become inured to losses.

Norman Gordon-Smith (VIIA D9)

Gordon-Smith was born on 31 August 1893 in Berlin. His mother resided in Montmartre, Paris. He went directly from the Royal Military College to the RFC at South Farnborough and was awarded his Royal Aero Club certificate, No. 1670, on 13 June 1915. His military flying training at Netheravon commenced later that month. Graduating at CFS on 23 August he was posted initially to 15 Squadron but then went to 12 Squadron three days later. On 6 September Gordon-

Norman Gordon-Smith

Smith crossed to France with the squadron and landed at St Omer. As with other units at this time they operated a motley collection of types, including RE5s, RE7s, Martinsyde S1 and BE2bs.

On 19 December 1915 he left on a reconnaissance in BE2c No. 2047 with Cunningham-Reid and failed to return.

Duncan Flower Cunningham-Reid (VIIA D8)

The visitor will notice that the headstone has the badge of his parent unit, the 29th Lancers, rather than the RAF or RFC emblem. The epitaph is also interesting in that it describes the action in which he was killed.

The son of Arthur and Agnes Reid of Gloucester Place, Kensington, London, Cunningham-Reid joined the RFC in October 1915 having served with the 29th Lancers (Deccan Horse).

Gordon-Smith and Cunningham-Reid were the second victory of Otto Parschau, a pilot with *Kampfgeschwader* 1. He ultimately claimed eight Allied machines and balloons and was awarded the *Pour le Mérite*. He is buried in St Quentin German Cemetery (*Cambrai* page 108). The two British airmen were initially buried in Oostcamp Churchyard but were later moved to Cement House.

D F Cunningham-Reid. His brother Alec earned a DFC with 85 Squadron RAF and was later an MP.

Continue ahead, then turn left for Ypres. This completes the first tour.

The wreckage of Cunningham-Reid and Gordon-Smith's machine. Otto Parschau is standing in front of the roundel on the wing.

The Central Area

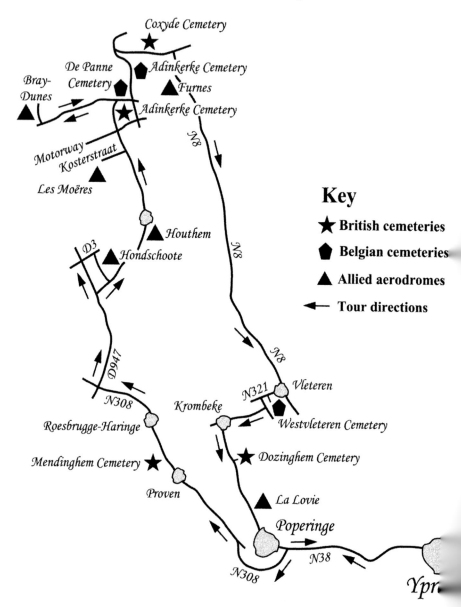

Coxyde Cemetery

Adinkerke Cemetery

De Panne Cemetery

Furnes

Bray-Dunes

Adinkerke Cemetery

N8

Motorway

Kosterstraat

Les Moëres

Houthem

D3

Hondschoote

N8

Key

★ **British cemeteries**

⬠ **Belgian cemeteries**

▲ **Allied aerodromes**

← **Tour directions**

D947

N308

Vleteren

N321

Roesbrugge-Haringe

Krombeke

Westvleteren Cemetery

Mendinghem Cemetery

Dozinghem Cemetery

Proven

La Lovie

Poperinge

N308

N38

Ypr

Chapter Two

THE CENTRAL AREA

Leave Ypres on the N38 towards Poperinge. Continue around Poperinge on the ring road (R33), and turn left at the T-junction at the end onto the N308 Proven. Follow the N308 over the roundabout and, just north of Proven village, the cemetery is visible, set back across a field to the left of the road. Turn left at the green CWGC sign to the cemetery.

Mendinghem Military Cemetery

This cemetery (No.43) was one of a group of burial grounds given popular names by the troops. The other two were Dozinghem and Bandaghem. In July 1916 the 46th (1st/1st Wessex) Casualty Clearing Station was established at Proven and this site was chosen as its cemetery. In July a further four CCS arrived, of which three remained until 1918. The cemetery was closed in September 1918 and today there are 2,391 Commonwealth graves and fifty-one German. Interestingly, the German graves have their backs to the rest of the headstones in the cemetery.

The first time I came here was on a very cold winter's afternoon. Someone had removed the register and I was forced to walk along each row of headstones in failing light searching for the graves I was interested in. By the time I had finished it was nearly dark and I was frozen to the marrow. It gave me a fair clue as to the conditions in the Ypres Salient trenches during the winter.

The first grave we are visiting is in Plot IX, which is the first on the right and is two-thirds of the way along the front row.

Robert Barton Cameron (IX B26)

This casualty lost his life in strange and sad circumstances. R B Cameron died on 7 January 1918 in an unexplained accident, which would seem to indicate suicide. At the Court of Inquiry examining the incident a number of witnesses were called.

Captain B U S Cripps stated:

> I command 'B' Flight of No. 9 Squadron, R.F.C., the deceased was an Observer in my Flight. He was detailed for Practice Contact Patrol in orders, the evening of January 6th, for 10 a.m. Jan. 7th. He should have reported to me at 9-30 a.m., Jan. 7th. This he did not do. At 10 a.m. I went to his Hut, and found him in bed asleep. I woke him up and asked him why he was not ready to leave the ground. He said he thought the weather was unsuitable, or words to that effect. I told him that I should have to see the Commanding Officer on the matter. I told him that I expected him to be at the shed within a quarter of an hour. At about 10-20 I saw him walking towards the Squadron Office. At about 10-30 as he had not arrived at the shed, I went to look for him, and found him coming out of the Intelligence Hut. I asked him what he was doing, and he replied that he was looking for a Contact Patrol Map. I told him that he had been instructed to copy the map himself the night before. He was then given his instructions and left the ground in R.E.8, No. 4460, Pilot Lt. Croden.

Second Lieutenant J E Croden stated:

> I am a pilot in 'B' Flight, No. 9 Squadron, R.F.C.; I was

9 Squadron group, R B Cameron is third from the left in the third row from the front.

detailed to do a Practice Contact Patrol on Jan. 7th., Lieut. R. B. Cameron was my Observer. At about 10-25 a.m. we left the ground. I took off in the usual manner and turned back over the aerodrome at a height of about 500 or 600 feet. I then turned to the left and flew straight to trim the machine. I looked in the mirror and saw Lt. Cameron standing up with his back towards me, I then looked at my instruments to trim the machine so as to fly at 600 feet. When I felt her shake and quiver, my control stick was jerked into my stomach. I then looked in the mirror to see what was happening and could not see Lieut. Cameron. I then glanced round and failing to see him then, I looked right down into the cock-pit, and found he was gone. I was about 200 yards North of No. 7 Squadron hangars when I made the discovery. He must have hit the elevator control wire in falling which would account for the control stick being jerked into my stomach.

Cameron landed on the edge of a ploughed field and his fall was observed by a Private R Selby, who was the first person at the scene. Cameron was found lying on his back and had been killed instantly. Selby enlisted the help of a number of his friends and the body was removed on a duck-board to their company headquarters where it was later collected by a 9 Squadron ambulance.

Cameron had been wounded twice when serving in the infantry and had told another officer in the squadron he had been in a serious crash while learning to fly. He sustained severe concussion and was in hospital for six months. Though there was no sign of the effects of this injury, according to other officers who knew him, this may have had a bearing on his conduct.

C M B Chapman (VI B1)

The next casualty we are visiting is located in the far left of the cemetery and is the first grave at the nearest end of the fourth row from the front. This was yet another fatality caused by German bombing of rear areas.

Charles Meredith Bouverie Chapman, whose father was a brewer, was born at Bridge in Kent on 9 January 1892. He was a lieutenant in the Buffs when he took his 'ticket' on 31 July 1915, No. 1491, at the London and Provincial School at Edgware. His military flying training was conducted at Shoreham and he was then posted to 22 Squadron. They had been formed on 1 September 1915 at Gosport in Hampshire and on 1 April 1916 he crossed to France with them, landing at St Omer. After a move to Vert Galand they settled at Bertangles where they remained for a year (*Somme* page 69).

Chapman was, however, not to remain with them for very long as on 23 May he was posted to B Flight of 24 Squadron, also based at Bertangles. He exchanged the lumbering FE2 for the diminutive and agile DH2 and, moreover, joined Lanoe Hawker VC's illustrious unit. While with 24 Squadron he claimed three victories, the first being on 22 June. On 4 August he returned to the UK having already earned a Military Cross in the short time he had spent in 24 Squadron. While at home he served in a number of training units and on 1 November 1916 was promoted to flight commander.

In this capacity he returned to France in May 1917 for duty with 29 Squadron at Le Hameau. They had

Major C M B Chapman, commanding 29 Squadron RFC.

exchanged their DH2s only a month or so earlier for the French Nieuport Scout. On 11 May he scored his first victory in his new unit, when an Albatros Scout was sent down out of control. His next victory on 11 June was unusual in that he brought it down on the Allied side of the lines.

In his combat report he wrote:

> *While on escort to a BE I saw 5 HA chasing a BE2e. I dived on one who turned east and fired about 30 rounds at 80 yards range. The HA turned west and appeared to lose control but regained it and again turned east. I fired another 30 rounds and he again turned west and started to land. I followed him down and saw him land at U19 Sheet 51B undamaged. He was taken prisoner by some infantry.*

The pilot was *Leutnant* Georg Simon of *Jasta* 11 and the machine, an Albatros DIII, was given the captured aircraft number G42. Simon, who was born on 4 January 1895, had joined *Jasta* 11 on 7 November 1916 but had been wounded on 29 January 1917.

Returning to his unit on 13 March he claimed one victory, a Bristol Fighter on 5 April 1917. This was the engagement when 48 Squadron flew the first Bristol Fighter sortie and had the misfortune to encounter the vastly experienced *Jasta* 11 led by Manfred von Richthofen. Four Bristols were lost, including the flight commander William Leefe-Robinson, who had earned the Victoria Cross in 1916 for destroying the German airship SLII (*Arras* page 174). Simon died on 5 November 1963.

Chapman was given command of 29 Squadron on 20 July 1917 and on 17 September claimed his seventh and last victory. He was made a *Chevalier de l'Ordre de Leopold* by the Belgians and also was awarded their *Croix de Guerre*.

On 1 October Chapman was killed in an attack on 29 Squadron's aerodrome at Poperinghe. Three air mechanics were killed with him and another, B W Payne, died the following day from his injuries.

The other casualties were:

Air Mechanic First Class Walter Hanbury Tracy (VI C17)
Air Mechanic First Class Arthur Wilfred Hall (VI C19)
Air Mechanic First Class Charles Walter Wingfield (VI C34)
Air Mechanic Second Class Benjamin Walter Payne (VII B3)

The final tragedy was the death of Chapman's brother William only six days later. He was a lieutenant observer in Charles' old unit, 22 Squadron, and was shot down in a Bristol Fighter.

Return to the N308 and turn left. Continue northwards, turning left in Roesbrugge Haringe to stay on the N308 Duinkerke. In Les Cinque Chemins, turn right at the roundabout on the D947 Hondschoote. After passing through the village of Hondschoote, turn right before the canal onto D3 Noordmeulen. At the next junction, as the road turns right carry on straight ahead (carefully!), and park beyond the farm buildings on your right.

Leutnant **Georg Simon's Albatros DIII of** *Jasta* **11.**

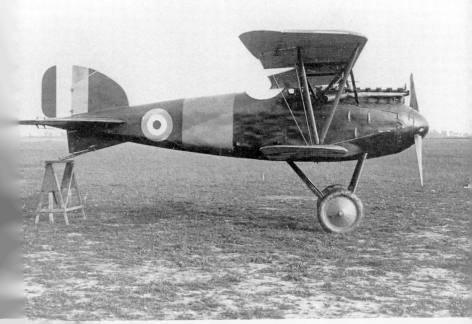

Hondschoote Aerodrome

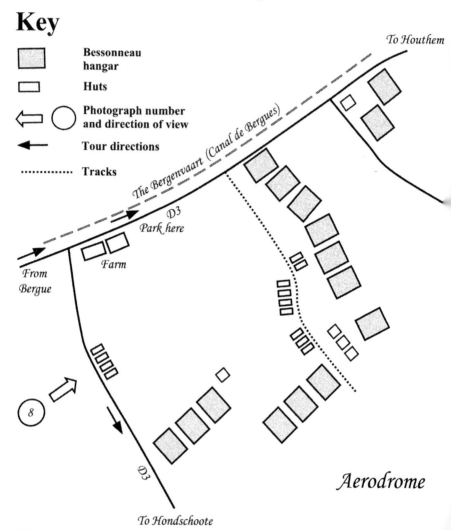

Key

- **Bessonneau hangar**
- **Huts**
- **Photograph number and direction of view**
- **Tour directions**
- **Tracks**

To Houthem

The Bergenvaart (Canal de Bergues)

D3
Park here

From Bergue

Farm

8

D3

To Hondschoote

Aerodrome

Note
The Bessonneaux are depicted as all the same dimensions.
However, they were a mixture of French and British manufacture.
The sizes were 20 x 20 metres, 20 x 28, 26 x 28 and 20 x 24.
This diagram depicts the northern part of the aerodrome and
there were almost certainly more hangars near to the village.

Hondschoote Aerodrome

This aerodrome was used mainly by the French, though both Belgian and British units were based here at one time or another.

However, our interest lies in a unique incident that occurred on 14 October 1918, when Second Lieutenant Ralph Talbot of the US Marine Corps landed on the airfield in order to save the life of his observer, Gunnery Sergeant Robert G Robinson, who had been seriously wounded. For the action in which they had just been involved both of them subsequently received the United States' highest award, the Medal of Honour.

The first Medal of Honour of the Great War was awarded for an incident that had aviation connections. On 17 October 1917 the USS *Huntington*, an armoured cruiser, was on an Atlantic convoy, and during the morning sent up a kite balloon. The balloon rose initially to 400 feet, but then the temperature dropped causing it to descend so that the basket fell into the sea and was dragged along. Patrick McGunigal, a Shipfitter First Class in the US Navy, courageously climbed down the side of the ship and rescued the observer.

Of the 123 Medals of Honour awarded during the First World War, only eight went to aviators, with two to the US Navy, two to the US Marine Corps and four to the Army Signal Corps (of which the US air service was a part). Of these eight, four were killed during the war and only two, Frank Luke and Erwin R Bleckley, are buried in Europe. For a full account of the Medal of Honour see *Airfields and Airmen: Verdun*, Meuse-Argonne American Cemetery.

Picture No.8. Hondschoote looking northeast in 2005.

The Northern Bombing Group

When the United States entered the war on 6 April 1917, the aviation element of the Marine Corps was very small, consisting of just seven officers, 43 other ranks and four aeroplanes. Over the next few months the organization expanded rapidly and was divided into two, the First Marine Aeronautic Company and the First Aviation Squadron. At the same time a number of officers were sent to Europe to report on how they could be employed along the North Sea coast. The primary target was the menace of the U-boat base at Bruges and the other ports, such as Zeebrugge and Ostend. Both the US Navy and Marine Corps were vying for their respective forces to control the operation and to reach a compromise the Navy Department authorised a special joint Navy-Marine organisation, which was designated the Northern Bombing Group (NBG).

The NBG was planned to consist of two wings – one day and one night, each having six squadrons, together with a supply and repair unit. The day wing was going to be marine and each squadron would operate eighteen American-built De Havilland DH4s. The night wing was a navy operation and each unit would have ten British Handley Page bombers. Unfortunately production of the two types was slow so the NBG was reduced to four squadrons per wing.

On 18 July 1918 three squadrons of the First Marine Aviation Force sailed from New York and arrived at Brest twelve days later. The last squadron arrived on 4 October. The navy Night Bombing Wing based Squadrons 1 and 2 at St Inglevert and 3 and 4 at Champagne. The marine units of the Day Bombing Wing utilized Oye, halfway between Calais and Dunkirk, for A and B Squadrons and La Fresne, southwest of Calais, for C and D Squadrons.

The non-delivery of the planned 72 US-manufactured DH4s meant that 54 DH9s were obtained from the British in exchange for American-built Liberty engines. In order to gain experience, marine crews were attached to 217 and 218 RAF Squadrons. One of the crews allocated to 218 Squadron was Ralph Talbot and Robert Robinson.

Ralph Talbot

Talbot was born on 6 January 1897 in South Weymouth, Massachusetts. Attending Weymouth High School, he excelled both athletically and academically and in the autumn of 1915 entered Mercersburg Academy in Pennsylvania. His abilities earned him a place at Yale University a year later. While serving in the college Artillery Training Corps he developed a passion for aviation and, as a consequence, enrolled at the Dupont Flying School at Wilmington,

Delaware. To further his interest he enlisted in the US Navy in October 1917 and was appointed to the rank of seaman second class. After ground training at the Massachusetts Institute of Technology and flying tuition in Florida, he was designated Naval Aviator No. 456.

Both the navy and marine forces were expanding rapidly, though the marines were having difficulty recruiting aviators. A number of navy pilots realised that they stood a better chance of being posted overseas if they joined the marines and so Talbot resigned from the navy and was appointed a second lieutenant in the Marine Corps Reserve on 18 May 1918. He arrived at the First Marine Aviation Force in Miami a week later and was assigned to Squadron C.

Ralph Talbot.

Both Talbot and his future gunner, Robinson, were part of the initial party which sailed from New York on 18 July 1918.

Robert G Robinson

Born on 30 April 1896 in Wayne, Michigan, Robinson enlisted in the Marine Corps on 22 May 1917 and was posted to the 92nd Marine Company at Quantico, Virginia. A month later he was attached to Squadron C of the First Marine Aviation Force and, after selection as a gunner, was sent to gunnery school in Ohio. Robinson, described as quietly spoken, but determined, finished his course and was graded as an expert rifleman, following which he was promoted to corporal.

The Medal of Honour flight

One of the first operations for Talbot and Robinson after their arrival in 218 Squadron RAF involved dropping supplies to Belgian and French troops who had run low on food and were unable to be re-supplied due to the unusable roads. A number

Robert G Robinson.

of RAF squadrons were employed dropping parcels, and in all thirteen tons were delivered. This was exceedingly dangerous work as it had to be carried out at very low altitude, and several machines were badly shot about. Talbot and Robinson flew a number of bombing operations as escort because their American-built DH4 was faster than the DH9s

Mechanics working on DH4 No. D-9 of the Northern Bombing Wing.

flown by 218 Squadron. As a result of their aggressive tactics on one occasion, when they shot down an enemy machine, they were commended by Major A A Cunningham, commander of the Marine Day Wing.

In the middle of October the pair returned to Squadron C at La Fresne. By this stage the Day Wing had finally received enough machines to mount their own operations. Thus on 14 October 1918 seven aeroplanes from Squadron C conducted the first all-marine mission of the Day Wing. This was the day the Allies recommenced their great offensive in Flanders and attacked along the whole length of the front from Dixmude to the River Lys. Retreating enemy troops and formations were harried and strafed all day, causing tremendous casualties. Several railway stations were bombed.

The Marine Day Wing target was the German railway centre at Thielt, twenty kilometres north of Courtrai. Eight machines, led by Captain Robert S Lytle, took off but one fell out with engine trouble. Over 2,000 pounds of bombs were dropped without incident but on the return flight they were intercepted by eleven enemy machines. This group split into two, with one flight attacking on the right side and the rest approaching the left. Despite their inexperience, Lytle wisely signalled his formation to close up and bring maximum gunfire to bear from the observers. They were able to fend off the German attack but, unfortunately, two machines left the safety of the formation due to engine trouble.

Of the two machines the Germans only harried one, that flown by Talbot and Robinson. A large number of enemy fighters latched on to it. Robinson fired a number of bursts at one, sending it down out of control. While thus engaged another two had positioned themselves below the DH4 and fired up through the cockpit floor. One bullet hit Robinson's elbow and all but severed his arm. Despite this he continued firing with only his right arm. His gun jammed and in an effort to relieve him Talbot attacked an enemy machine using his front guns. These too jammed but Robinson was able to clear his stoppage and continue the fight. Shortly he was wounded twice more, once in the stomach and once in the thigh. At this point he collapsed but landed on the aeroplane's control cables, making the machine difficult for Talbot to fly. Though his guns were jammed Talbot flew his machine at an enemy scout in such an aggressive manner that it was forced to retreat.

This manoeuvre gave Talbot the chance to evade his attackers and by diving to low level he escaped, crossing the lines at only a height of about 50 feet. Knowing his observer was wounded he flew to Hondschoote, where a field hospital was located. Robinson was rushed to the hospital where not only was his life preserved but the Belgian surgeon also saved his arm.

In spite of the damage to his machine, Talbot returned to La Fresne alone later in the day. His machine was patched up and over the next few days participated in a number of raids. On 25 October Talbot and Second Lieutenant Colgate W Darden Jr. attempted to test the engine of a worn-out DH4. On the first abortive take off the machine failed to get airborne. On the second they only reached three feet when they hit an embankment alongside a bomb trench at the end of the aerodrome. The undercarriage was ripped off and the machine flipped over and crashed into a heap of bombs. Darden was thrown clear though he was severely injured.

The machine burst into flames with Talbot being trapped beneath the engine. Several men courageously carried bombs away from the scene. Though badly burned it is almost certain that his death was caused by the engine crushing him. Talbot was buried on 29 October in the British cemetery at Les Baraques in Plot 5, Row B, Grave No. 3. This plot no longer exists as all the US graves were removed after the war and today the visitor will notice the large gap where they used to be. Talbot's body was later removed to his home town of South Weymouth, Massachusetts.

His Medal of Honour was awarded on Armistice Day 1920. The citation reads:

For exceptionally meritorious service and extraordinary heroism while attached to Squadron C, First Marine Aviation Force, in France. Second Lieutenant Talbot participated in numerous air raids into enemy territory. On 8 October 1918, while on such a raid, he was attacked by nine enemy scouts, and in the fight that followed shot down an enemy plane. Also, on 14

October 1918 while on a raid over Pittham, Belgium, Lieutenant Talbot and another plane became detached from the formation on account of motor trouble, and were attacked by 12 enemy scouts. During the severe fight that followed, his plane shot down one of the enemy scouts. His observer was shot through the elbow and his gun jammed. Second Lieutenant Talbot maneuvered to gain time for his observer to clear the jam with one hand, and then returned to the fight. The observer fought until shot twice, once in the stomach and once in the hip. When he collapsed, Lieutenant Talbot attacked the nearest enemy scout with his front guns and shot him down. With his observer unconscious and his motor failing, he dived to escape the balance of the enemy and crossed the German trenches at an altitude of 50 feet, landing at the nearest hospital to leave his observer, and then returning to his aerodrome.

A US Navy destroyer was named after Ralph Talbot in October 1936 and commissioned at Charlestown Navy Yard.

Robinson's citation is the same as Talbot's. He was transferred to the US Naval Hospital at Brest in November 1918 and thence to the Marine Barracks in New York during January 1919. He was discharged in June 1919 and appointed a second lieutenant in the Marine Corps Reserve. Finally retiring in 1923 he made his home at St Ignace, Michigan. In 1971 the Robert G Robinson Award was initiated for the best annual Marine Flight Officer of the Year. He died on 5 October 1974 and is buried in Arlington National Cemetery, Virginia.

Much of this information has been taken from an excellent book, *Medal of Honor Aviators of World War One* by Alan E Durkota (see Further Reading section).

Return to the junction, and turn left back to Hondschoote. In the village, turn left at D3 Furnes, then left onto D55 Furnes. Just before entering Houthem village, look for a drive entrance to a farm on the right. Park.

Houthem Aerodrome

After their occupation by the Germans the Belgians were left with just a tiny corner of their country. For nearly four years the village of Houthem became the capital of free Belgium and as such was a heaving scene of activity. The headquarters of the Belgian army was on

Houthem Aerodrome

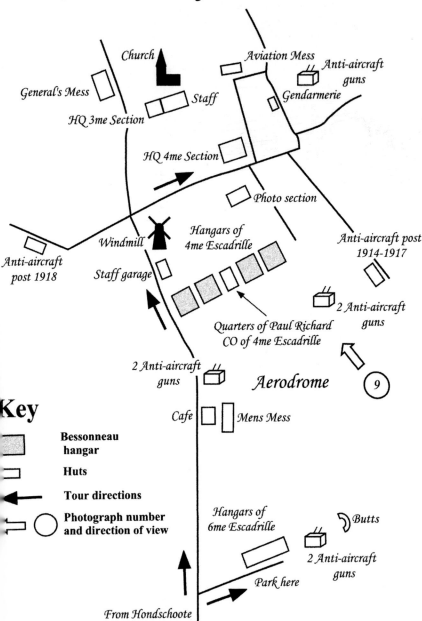

Church

Aviation Mess

Anti-aircraft guns

General's Mess

Staff

Gendarmerie

HQ 3me Section

HQ 4me Section

Photo section

Anti-aircraft post 1914-1917

Windmill

Hangars of 4me Escadrille

Anti-aircraft post 1918

Staff garage

2 Anti-aircraft guns

Quarters of Paul Richard CO of 4me Escadrille

2 Anti-aircraft guns

Aerodrome

9

Key

Cafe

Mens Mess

Bessonneau hangar

Huts

Tour directions

Photograph number and direction of view

Hangars of 6me Escadrille

Butts

2 Anti-aircraft guns

Park here

From Hondschoote

Picture No.9. Houthem viewed in 2005 from the south.

the edge of the aerodrome and King Albert and the royal family lived nearby. The front line was only seventeen kilometres to the east and the French border three kilometres to the west.

The fact the aerodrome was so close to the French frontier was a bonus as the Belgians would take a big-bellied Farman F40 to the French aerodrome at Hondschoote and load up with crates of alcohol for the squadron, which was in contravention of orders from High Command!

The initial aerodromes employed by the *AMB* once the front line had stabilised were Coxyde/Furnes (page 123) where I, II and III *Escadrilles* were based, and Houthem where the IV and V *Escadrilles* were established. There was also a seaplane unit at Calais.

Willy Coppens, Belgium's highest scoring ace, after completing his pilot training at Étampes, in early 1916 was posted to *6me Escadrille* at Houthem where he was to fly the Royal Aircraft Factory BE2c. He described his arrival in his book *Days on the Wing*:

Willy Coppens in front of his Hanriot HD1. The thistle was the unit insignia of the 1ère *Escadrille* which in March 1918 was re-numbered the 9me *Escadrille*.

Leaving my kit in the station, I climbed on to a lorry proceeding in the direction of Houthem. Travelling thus, I covered that long, straight road, bordered on either side by willow trees, past an endless succession of low-lying meadows, separated by endless dykes. My lorry deposited me at some distance from the village. A very severe spell of weather had set in, and the country was deep in snow. It was bitterly cold. I stepped out briskly, glowing inwardly with ambition and hope, and at last certain of the immediate future – even though I was not on my way to a Fighter Squadron.

As night drew in and I approached Houthem, the village stood out in dim silhouette against the dark wintry sky – the low-built houses, following the main street in its Z-shaped course past the church, just visible on my right, and, beyond, the windmill, with its sails outstretched in a broad cross above the mound it stood on, and the yellow shafts of light escaping through the rifts in the doors and the shuttered windows. Dark shadows lay on the snow, and my feet sank at every step and made no sound.

At Houthem I lived in a cosy little room in the village that I had decorated with brightly-coloured cretonne. I had naturally tapped the electric current serving our G.H.Q., and my quarters were exceedingly comfortable. Even so, I was later to grow much fonder of my little room at Les Moëres, by the side of the aerodrome. An aviator must live in the shadow of his shed to enjoy life and get the best out of his calling. The dispersal of the pilots at Houthem was fatal to the corporate spirit, and as a result the Squadron was divided against itself. The squadrons at Les Moëres possessed much more esprit de corps.

At Houthem, almost all the officers of the Squadron – therefore too many – shared a common mess, a vast, unattractive hall. A small minority lived in the junior mess, also known as the Potinière, which was established in a wooden building on the other side of the village.

Belgian General Headquarters had established themselves at Houthem, wishing in their innocence to have an aerodrome close by for their defence. They showed less keenness for this defence when the Germans came across and bombed the aerodrome, and I know of many pilots who were subsequently able to gain possession of the best rooms in the village...

At conference time, Houthem was as animated as an anthill;

the High Street was full of cars and officers greeted one another cheerily. But it did not last long, and as soon as the meeting was over, the village relapsed into slumber. The flying men were all in their various messes, and all was quiet save for an occasional outburst following some high-spirited 'rag'. The G.H.Q. officers, although more numerous, were conscious of their position, and therefore made less noise. They never came near us. They were divided according to their rank, into three messes, one for the juniors, one for the officers of Field rank, and the third for General Officers. Their colleagues in the army called these messes the 'Hospital', the 'Asylum', and the 'Mortuary'.

In April 1917 Coppens was transferred to the 4*me Escadrille*, also based at Houthem and still flying two-seater reconnaissance machines. While here he was able to fly the Nieuport scout which belonged to Commandant Hagemans, the commander of the centre at Houthem.

On 15 July 1917 Coppens realised his ambition to become a fighter pilot when he was posted to 1*ère Escadrille* based at Les Moëres. They were commanded by *Commandant* Fernand Jacquet and operated Nieuport scouts.

Continue through the village, and turn right for Adinkerke. Follow the road which eventually runs dead straight for some distance. After passing a crossroads about halfway along the straight, look for a yellow road sign Adinkerke De Panne. Turn left at the road sign into Kosterstraat. Continue past St. Gonzalve Farm, the only farm to the left of the road, and park at the first corner beyond it.

Les Moëres Aerodrome

This aerodrome is associated with the formation of the Belgian *Groupe de Chasse* and Belgium's greatest fighter pilot, Willy Coppens. He claimed all of his thirty-seven victories while based here.

The site of Les Moëres was taken over when the aerodrome at Furnes (page 123) became untenable due to shelling by heavy calibre German guns.

Coppens described the aerodrome:

From the point of view of an aerodrome, the place was far from being ideal as it stood, and a considerable amount of work was necessary to reclaim the marshy land, on which the squadron had made its home, before it was really fit for use. This

Les Moëres Aerodrome

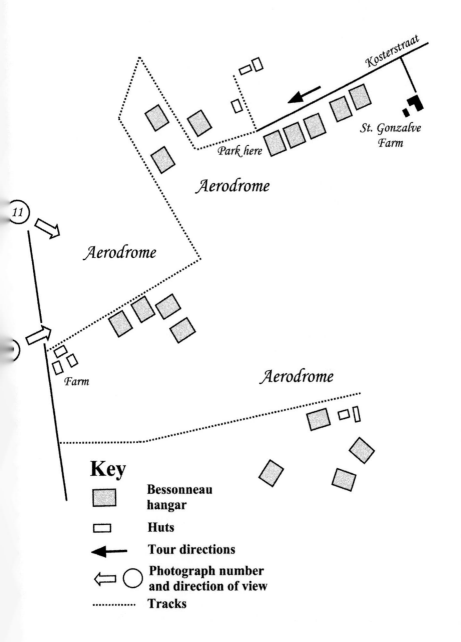

Kosterstraat

St. Gonzalve Farm

Park here

Aerodrome

Aerodrome

11

Aerodrome

Farm

Aerodrome

Key

Bessonneau hangar

Huts

Tour directions

Photograph number and direction of view

Tracks

Picture No.10. Les Moëres looking northeast in 2005.

flat country is criss-crossed by ruler-straight roads, intersecting at right-angles. These roads are lined with gaunt willow-trees whose grizzled, long-haired heads frown sullenly across the low-lying landscape, and are separated from the fields that lie alongside them by dykes that are both wide and deep.

A road, identical with every other road, leading to two

Picture No. 11. The aerodrome looking southeast in the First World War.

isolated farms in Les Moëres, finished up at one corner of the aerodrome. Here, away from all traffic, the green canvas sheds and the various buildings housing the squadron had been erected. The first wooden hut one reached sheltered the mess, and next to this stood another, which was partitioned off into ten cubicles occupied by ten pilots, with a hall in the centre. Additional living accommodation was provided by two large aeroplane-cases (originally used for the transport of Sopwith two-seaters), each the size of a railway-carriage, and each subdivided into three little cubicles opening direct on to the aerodrome. These cases and huts stood in line, in the shade of a row of willows, alongside a dyke, where the wind, bringing with it the fragrance of the dunes, used to come and sigh among the reeds.

The mess had six windows. In front of each of these was arranged a table to seat four, giving the whole the appearance of a dining car. Chairs of light oak upholstered in green velvet, found in an abandoned villa at Coxyde, added to our comfort, and a piano, at which André De Meulemeester sat for hours at a stretch – for De Meulemeester was a born pianist of very great skill – lent a note of gaiety that was greatly appreciated.

The *Groupe de Chasse*

In March 1918 there was a reorganization of the *AMB*, when a dedicated fighter wing was formed. Prior to this, fighter pilots were called out to escort two-seater machines, or for offensive patrols at the request of a ground unit or at the individual pilot's initiative.

Despite the rigid Belgian army policy of promotion by seniority, King Albert insisted that Fernand Jacquet became the commanding officer over the heads of more senior officers. His confidence was well-rewarded as Jacquet welded it into an effective force, although limited in numbers and still operating a number of types that were obsolescent.

A little of tradition was lost in this reorganisation, as the 1ère *Escadrille* became the 9me, the 5me *Escadrille* was re-numbered the 10me and a new unit, the 11me, was formed. The *Groupe de Chasse* established itself on Les Moëres. Nominally the 9me operated the Hanriot HD1, the 10me the Spad and the 11me the Camel.

Willy Coppens and the Hanriot

Born on 6 July 1892 at Watermaal-Bosvoorde, near Brussels, Willy Omer François Jean Coppens started the war with the 1ère *Regiment Grenadiers*. Like a number of Belgian aviators, he learned to fly in the

UK and received his Royal Aeronautical Club certificate, No. 2140, on 9 December 1915. Following further training at the Belgian Aviation School at Étampes he joined 6*me Escadrille* in April 1917. Initially he flew Nieuport scouts in the 1*ère Escadrille* but shortly a new type of machine arrived. Coppens again:

> I was present when the first Hanriots came, and on this occasion I can assert that the Squadron very nearly refused them, as I believe it had refused the Spads.
>
> André de Meulemeester had the first and declined to keep it. He therefore handed it over to Olieslagers, who declined to keep that which De Meulemeester had no use for. And so on, and I, being about the last to have joined the squadron, finally had it offered to me. I fell in love with the Hanriot at first sight. It was light as a feather on the controls, and the pilot had a wonderfully clear field of vision.
>
> The Hanriot was extremely easy to handle and pleasant to fly. It was strong in spite of its apparent fragility, and was faster and climbed better than the Nieuport.

The HD1 was designed by Emile Eugène Dupont for René Hanriot's company in the summer of 1916. Proof tests were carried out on it in January 1917. Unfortunately, though it was a good design, the excellent Spad was just coming into large scale production. Also the Hanriot employed the same engine as the Nieuport scout, which the French were trying to replace, and was not enough of an improvement over the Nieuport to warrant production for the French air service. However, it was tested by the Italians who adopted it as the principal replacement for their Nieuports. A total of 1,700 served with the Italian air service, of which about half were built in Italy under licence.

The Belgians ordered 125 HD1s, the first being delivered on 22 August 1917. The enthusiasm Coppens displayed for the type eventually persuaded the doubters, and the 1*ère Escadrille* was fully equipped with them. The Hanriot would soldier on into the mid-1920s with both the Italians and Belgians.

On 22 August 1917 Coppens became the first Belgian to fly a Hanriot on an operational sortie. During the latter part of the year he made three claims but they were unconfirmed. On 25 April 1918 he obtained his first confirmed victory, when he shot down a two-seater, which crashed near Ramscapelle. The great disadvantage with the Hanriot was that it was only fitted with one fixed Vickers machine gun. Coppens was able to obtain twenty rounds of incendiary ammunition and on 8 May he attacked a German observation balloon and brought it down. This was the first kite balloon shot down by a Belgian pilot. Just under two hours later he brought another down in flames. After each of his victories, in his enthusiasm, he gave an impromptu aerobatic display, much to the enjoyment of the Belgian frontline troops.

From this moment Coppens specialised in attacking observation balloons. These were difficult and dangerous targets and many pilots avoided them. On 22 July he shot down three when he had been poaching on the British part of the front. This was frowned upon by Belgian General Headquarters but a reprimand was avoided when the British awarded him a Military Cross for the feat! By the first week in October 1918 Coppens had claimed 33 balloons and become the most successful 'balloon buster' of any nation.

On the morning of 14 October he took off with Etienne Hage to destroy a balloon near Vladslo. Coppens again:

> I soon caught sight of the Thourout kite-balloon, 'flying' at about 1,800 feet, and at the same time I saw another at 2,100 feet, over Praet-Bosch. The latter balloon was the higher, and would therefore require to be attacked after the first – which would have to be taken by surprise, as quickly as possible, before it was pulled down too far.
>
> At 6 a.m., I fired four rounds into the Praet-Bosch balloon now at a height of 2,400 feet, and the envelope began to burn.
>
> Etienne Hage failed to see the flames, and instead of following me, went back to the balloon, while the ground defences fired at us for all they were worth, and the Thourout balloon, warned, started to go down.
>
> Turning back towards Thourout, and flying – so far unscathed – through that maelstrom of incendiary projectiles from the 'onion' batteries below, I pondered on my chances of getting through.
>
> At 6.5 a.m., I sailed in to open fire on the Thourout balloon, now hauled down to 900 feet, and in addition to the bursting of the shells, I heard the vicious bark of the small-calibre machine guns. I was 450 feet away, when I felt a terrible blow on the left leg.
>
> An incendiary bullet, after passing through the thin planking of the floor, had struck my shin-bone, smashing everything in its

passage and inflicting a wound all the more painful for the fact that the bullet, being hollow, had flattened, becoming in effect a 'dum-dum' bullet. The muscles were torn apart, the bone shattered, and the artery cut in half.

Because of the shock and pain Coppen's right leg went rigid, pushing the rudder bar, which caused the machine to yaw and enter a spin. At the same time his hand involuntarily clutched the trigger control, firing his machine-gun and hosing the bullets in all directions, a few hitting the balloon and setting it on fire. Fortunately his rudder bar had a foot strap at either end, so he was able to control it using only his

Jan Olieslagers in his Nieuport Scout. The 'Antwerp Devil' claimed six enemy machines and another sixteen unconfirmed claims. He flew the greatest number of fighter patrols in the *AMB* – a total of 518. He died in 1942, aged only 58. See next page.

undamaged right foot. He turned for the safety of the Belgian front line.

A sweat on my forehead made me snatch down my goggles, so that they remained hanging round my neck, and pull off my fur-lined cap. I had done all my flying at the front with this cap, and nothing would have parted me from it; with an effort, I stuffed it under my coat. On the other hand, I tore off and shed my silk muffler protecting my face from the cold. I wanted air, ice-cold air, to bathe my face and keep me from fainting.

Crossing the lines Coppens put his machine down in a small field by the side of a road, where the weakened undercarriage collapsed. He was quickly removed from his Hanriot and transferred to the hospital at La Panne, where he was operated on. For several days he suffered from terrible pain and fever. King Albert visited him twice and on the second visit insisted that the doctors amputate Coppens' leg in order to save his life. While in hospital the Armistice was signed and he was transferred to hospital in Brussels, until finally discharged in July 1919.

As befitted his position as Belgium's most successful fighter pilot he was heavily decorated, being made an *Officier de l'Ordre de Leopold,* an *Officier de l'Ordre de la Couronne* and received the *Croix de Guerre* with twenty-seven palms and thirteen *Lion Vermeils,* plus twenty-eight citations. In addition he received the British DSO and the Serbian Order of the White Eagle. After the war he became a Baron and was persuaded by King Albert to remain in the army. This was a decision he came to regret, as he spent most of his years as a military attaché in Italy, France, Switzerland and Great Britain, receiving little promotion. He left the army in 1940, still only a major. During the Second World War he lived in Switzerland, organising resistance work, but in the late 1960s returned to Belgium. For the last five years of his life he resided with the only daughter of Jan Olieslagers, Belgium's fifth most successful fighter pilot of the Great War, until his death on 21 December 1986.

Return to the main road and turn left. Pass over the motorway and turn left at the T-junction. Continue along the road (the N39 in Belgium, becoming the N1 after the French border), until turning right over the canal bridge for Bray-Dunes. Park beyond the supermarket on the right hand side.

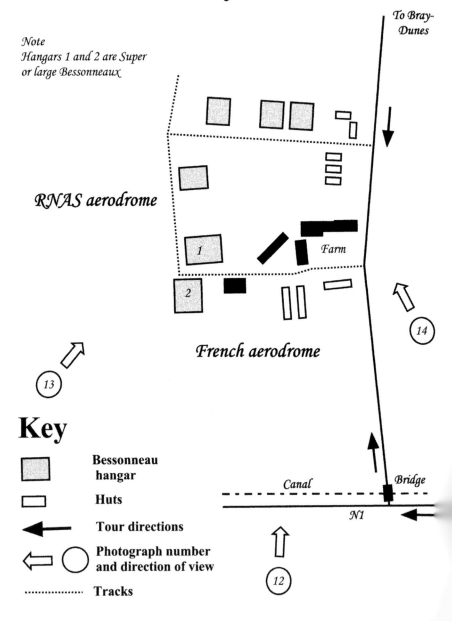

Bray-Dunes
Frontier Aerodrome

To Bray-Dunes

Note
Hangars 1 and 2 are Super
or large Bessonneaux

RNAS aerodrome

Farm

1

2

French aerodrome

13

14

Key

Bessonneau hangar

Huts

Tour directions

Photograph number and direction of view

Tracks

Canal

Bridge

N1

12

Bray-Dunes Aerodrome

This aerodrome was employed by both the British and French air services. The first RFC squadron, No. 52, arrived on 15 June 1917. However it is more readily associated with units of the Royal Naval Air Service, in particular 3 Naval, who spent from September to November 1917 and January to March 1918 based here. Other units which served at this spot during different periods were 1 Naval, 4 Naval, 8 Naval and 9 Naval. RFC/RAF squadrons were 34, 48, 52, 54, 65 and 92. Initially the site was known as the Frontier Aerodrome, as it sat on the French/Belgian border. Later it was increased in size by taking up the large, flat area to the west and this was known as the Middle Aerodrome. In official documents it is frequently difficult to work out which aerodrome is being referred to. The same family, the Dewittes, cultivate the farm today as in the First World War.

A number of famous aces served in 3 Naval, such as J S T Fall, F C Armstrong, H F Beamish, L S Breadner, J D Breakey, A W Carter, A B Ellwood, R A Little (*Arras* page 166), J J Malone, L H 'Tich' Rochford and A T Whealy (*Arras* page 124).

It was unusual for an enemy machine to land intact on the Allied side and even rarer for a squadron to retain it for any length of time. After the war it was quite common for units to 'acquire' enemy machines and fly them. But during hostilities this was virtually unheard of, except perhaps for the unique incident involving a machine captured by 3 Naval. The RNAS did not have the G number system for captured German aeroplanes, as was used by the RFC, for technical

Picture No.12. Bray-Dunes looking north in 2000.

Picture No.13. Bray-Dunes Frontier Aerodrome during the First World War looking northeast.

Picture No.14. Bray-Dunes looking north. The nearest hangars are most likely the French aerodrome and the ones at the top belong to the RNAS.

analysis. Tich Rochford wrote of the incident from late 1917 in his autobiography *I Chose the Sky:*

I am sure that the pilots concerned must experience a special feeling of elation when they have forced an enemy aircraft to land intact on their own side of the lines. Thus it happened that during the evening of 10th September, Flight Lieutenant Redpath when leading 'A' Flight on an FPP, intercepted a two-seater DFW which was returning at about 15,000 feet from a reconnaissance flight. Redpath and his flight attacked and forced it to land intact in a field between Furnes and Adinkerke. The pilot was unhurt but the observer was wounded and died later in hospital. Breadner, who was still our acting CO in the absence of Mulock, sent out a party with CPO Finch to dismantle the DFW and bring it back to Bray Dunes that same evening. There were several bullet holes in the wings and fuselage and one through the radiator but the damage was not really very serious and within a few days it had all been repaired and, the British roundels having replaced the German crosses on the fuselage and planes, we were able to fly it.

The captured DFW remained with us at Bray Dunes for two weeks. All our pilots flew it and some did so on several occasions. On each flight we usually took with us in the observer's cockpit two members of the ground staff and eventually everyone had a joyride in it. After the Sopwith Camel, the DFW was a very cumbersome aeroplane to handle. The controls were heavy to operate, the lateral control being particularly bad in this respect. However, the big water-cooled Benz engine seemed exceptionally good and ran extremely smoothly. Eventually orders were received to deliver it to RNAS Dover.

We drew lots to decide who should be the pilot and observer on this trip and I got the lucky card for pilot and Harry Chisam that for observer. Our Armament Officer had a machine-gun fitted to the mounting in the observer's cockpit so that Harry could warn off any enthusiastic scout pilot who might not see the British markings and think he had an easy Hun to shoot down in the Channel.

It was 12.45 pm on 24th September when I took off from Bray Dunes with Harry Chisam in the DFW. I flew along the coast, gradually climbing, towards Calais where, at 9,000 feet, I turned seawards and made for Dover. Nothing unusual happened until

The Camels of B Flight, 9 Naval, on the Middle Aerodrome.

we were near the English coast when a Sopwith Camel approached and circled round us several times. Once or twice he dived on us but it was obvious that he realized we were not an EA and knew of the signal that had been sent out before we left Bray Dunes informing all concerned of the necessary details of this flight, and eventually he left us. We landed at Dover after a flight of about one hour, handed over the DFW and collected a couple of Sopwith Camels to deliver to Dunkirk.

Though he writes that the observer died of his injuries, evidence suggests that the crew of *Vizefeldwebel* Friedrich Eckardt (pilot) and *Leutnant* Franz Adolf Gilge of *FA(A)* 293b both survived.

The DFW captured by 3 Naval, and flown to England by 'Tich' Rochford.

Leonard Henry 'Tich' Rochford

'Tich' was born on 10 November 1893 in Enfield, Essex and tried to join the RNAS at the start of the war but was too young. Learning to fly with the London and Provincial Flying Club at Hendon, he received his 'ticket', No. 1840 on 7 October 1915. He joined the RNAS in May 1916 and after a period of training was posted to 3 Naval in January 1917. Flying the Sopwith Pup Tich claimed his first German machine on 4 May 1917 when he sent an Albatros scout down out of control.

In his introduction to Tich's autobiography, the great Canadian ace Ray Collishaw (page 194) wrote;

'Tich' Rochford.

Tich was a truly remarkable person. He stood only a bit over five feet tall and I think I could have worn him for a watch charm. He had a quiet, gentle and unassuming manner but when he got into the cockpit of a fighter he was absolute hell on wings. No one would suspect that inside such a tiny frame was such a heart of a lion. Not unless they'd seen Tich in action as I did many times.

Tich claimed three enemy machines flying the Pup before the squadron was issued with the legendary Camel. In 1918 he knocked down German machines at a steady rate and by the end of the war had claimed a total of twenty-nine victories though, as with most pilots, some of these were shared with other members of his flight. He was 3 Naval/203 Squadron's most successful pilot and received the DSC and Bar, the DFC and was Mentioned in Despatches.

Unlike the RFC, the RNAS had no set length tour of duty. It was left to the discretion of the commanding officer to decide when an aircrew member had had enough and post him home for a rest. Tich managed to remain with 203 Squadron (as it had become on 1 April 1918, with the formation of the RAF) for nearly two years – an amazing length of front line service. At the Armistice he was the sole survivor of those who had joined with him in January 1917 and had flown an incredible total of 742 operational hours – treble the average RFC tour of duty. On leaving France he wrote in his logbook:

Left No. 203 Squadron on the 9th December 1918 after being

*with them since 24th January 1917. I shall always remember
those two years as among the happiest of my life. At all times we
were all a happy family and stuck together through thick and
thin.*

In April 1919 he left the RAF and between the wars worked in
engineering, then as a farmer. Called up in the Second World War, he
resumed flying in 1941 after a refresher course, and served until
demobilized in June 1945. Retiring to Somerset, he was an active
member of *Cross and Cockade* until his death on 17 December 1986.

**Return to the canal bridge, and turn left on the N1 to Adinkerke. In
Adinkerke, look for the green CWGC sign on the left, just after the
footbridge over the canal. Turn right down the side road opposite to
the cemetery sign.**

Adinkerke Military Cemetery

This cemetery is No. 16 in the Commonwealth War Graves
Commission handbook. From June to November 1917 the area from
the Belgian coast to St Georges was held by the British XV Corps. Two
casualty clearing stations, Nos. 24 and 39, were established near
Oosthoek and, in addition, No. 1 Canadian CCS was here for a short
time. As a result of the German invasion of 1940 further casualties
were buried here, including a number of aircrew from the later years of
the Second World War. One of these, Squadron Leader J C Mungo-
Park, is buried in the centre of the cemetery in grave E17. He was a
well-known Battle of Britain pilot and had received a DFC and Bar,
having claimed a dozen victories by the time he was killed on 27 June
1941, while in command of 74 Squadron.

The casualty we have come to visit is the second from the end of the
row on your left as you enter the cemetery. The adjacent grave (G1), A
J Chadwick, figures in an incident in the next section.

Francis Dominic Casey (G2)
The son of Maurice and Agnes Casey of Clonmel, County
Tipperary, Ireland, he was born on 3 August 1890. Joining the RNAS
on 28 May 1916, he flew as an observer with 2 Wing. After pilot tuition
at Eastchurch, Casey completed his training at Cranwell and was
posted initially to 1 Wing, then to 3 Naval Squadron at Dunkirk. Here,
as previously mentioned, he joined an illustrious unit, containing

several notable naval aces. While at Dover he had been assessed as *Perhaps too dashing, always sets a good example to his fellow flyers.*

Again referring to *I Chose the Sky,* the autobiography of Tich Rochford, he wrote:

F D Casey, accidentally killed 10 August 1917.

Among our pilots the Irishman Francis Casey was an interesting and amusing character. Before becoming a pilot he had been an observer. As such he had flown for a considerable time with Red Mulock in the RNAS Dunkirk Command and there was a very close bond of friendship between them. Like many of his countrymen Casey had to have a particular pet grouse which, in his case, was the delay in his promotion to the rank of Flight Lieutenant. At regular intervals, his temper reaching a high pitch, he would write out a letter of resignation and hand it into the CO's office. Mulock, who understood Casey through and through, would shelve the letter, or more likely tear it up and throw it in the fire. There the matter would rest until Casey's anger was roused again.

He had a fund of amusing stories some of which are unprintable, but there are two which I think are worth repeating. The first concerns the time Casey, stationed at Dunkirk, was the observer in a Nieuport two-seater flown by a pilot who shall be nameless. They had been ordered to carry out a photographic reconnaissance flight to an objective some miles behind the German lines. When they reached the lines near Nieuport on the Belgian coast the pilot stopped short as if afraid to cross into enemy territory. Several times he flew around in circles but never once crossed the lines. Eventually Casey's patience became exhausted.

Now, in the Nieuport two-seater the pilot's and observer's cockpits were not separated by a solid partition and the observer could stretch his legs under the pilot's seat. Casey waited until the pilot next turned towards the lines and as soon as he reached them he pushed his leg under the pilot's seat and pressed his foot against the base of the control stick. The Nieuport started to dive and the more the pilot attempted to pull back the stick so Casey

Sopwith Pup N6183 of 3 Naval. It also served with 11 Naval and after a ditching in the sea on 14 August 1917 it was deleted.

pushed his foot more firmly against it until the Nieuport steepened its dive to near vertical.

Thinking something was wrong with the controls the pilot became frantic and used all his strength to pull back the stick, but without success. At last, when Casey judged the earth was rushing up towards them rather too quickly, he gradually decreased his pressure on the stick and the pilot was able to level out at about 100 feet altitude on the enemy side of the lines. With perspiration streaming from his brow he turned westwards and headed for Dunkirk at full speed. He never discovered that Casey had been the cause of his panic.

The second story concerns a later period when Casey had become a pilot, the incident taking place at Dover. The other pilot involved, who was the same one as in the previous story, was about to take off in a Bristol Scout when Casey, in an Avro, landed at right-angles to him and cut off the tail of his machine. The Bristol Scout, its engine revving at full speed, spun round like a top and finally crashed. The Station Commander rushed out onto the aerodrome in his car and, noticing that the pilot of the Bristol Scout looked very shaken, remarked to him that his face was very pale. Back came the reply: 'Yes Sir, my face is white with rage but not with fear.'

At this time 3 Naval were operating the Sopwith Pup and on 17 March 1917 Casey claimed his first victory, a Halberstadt DII. By 2 May he had claimed a total of nine enemy machines, been awarded the DSC and was Mentioned in Despatches. On 3 June he was appointed a flight commander.

Tich Rochford again:

> On 11th August Francis Casey was killed. He had been on leave in England and returned to Furnes on the evening of the previous day. Soon after breakfast he took up his Camel and, as was usual with him, commenced doing 'stunts' at a very low altitude. He did side-loops and spins each time pulling out of the dive just above the ground. Eventually he put his machine into a spin at a height too low from which to recover and he crashed in a field across the road which ran past the aerodrome. He was unconscious when put on a stretcher and into the ambulance which took him to the hospital in La Panne where he was operated on at once for a fracture of the base of the skull. He died in the afternoon and that same evening was buried in the cemetery at Coxyde. We all attended the burial service which was conducted by the RC padre from Dunkirk and Wing Commander Mulock, Casey's great friend, also came along from Dunkirk. I noticed he left two wreaths by the graveside. One was from himself and the other from Kathryn Martyn, a young actress who was then in one of the London shows and to whom, I believe, Casey was engaged.

I think Casey epitomises a modern flying saying or idiom – *There are old pilots and bold pilots but there aren't any old, bold pilots.*

Return to the main road and turn right. At the roundabout, turn left over the canal bridge into Adinkerke. Look for the church on the left hand side of the road, and turn left down the side street immediately beyond the church to the cemetery behind. You may see small signs to the Belgian Military Cemetery marking the turn.

Adinkerke Belgian Cemetery

All the different nationalities that have cemeteries on the Western Front have their own style and the Belgians are no exception. The headstones are very distinctive with the black, yellow and red plaque at the top and the bronze details on the front. There are 1,720 graves here, including several Britons.

There are six members of the *Aviation Militaire Belge (AMB)* buried here. One, L C E de M d'Opstaele, has a non-standard headstone. Unfortunately for the battlefield visitor and the historian, many of the Belgian casualties were removed after the war and returned to their home towns. The flying casualties interred here, together with their grave numbers, are:

Andre M Smits (419). Crashed into the sea 13 March 1916.

Leonard Charles Etienne de Maelcamp d'Opstaele (735). Killed in a flying accident, 22 August 1917.

Fernand de Woot de Trixhe (740). Killed in a flying accident, 31 May 1917.

Paul E de Goussancourt (741). Hit by a shell and killed, 12 May 1917.

Paul Charles Gustave Hanciau (743). Died of wounds, 30 September 1917.

Edouard Herman (787). Shot down and killed, 23 October 1917.

Sergent Baron Fernand de Woot de Trixhe (740)

Two of the Belgian graves are of particular interest. The first one (740) we have come to visit is situated along the central aisle beyond the second circular area of grass, and is halfway down on the left hand side.

After the German occupation, the Belgians were left with a very small corner of their homeland. There was only enough room for operational aerodromes and they would have been too close to the front line for training purposes anyway. Thus most Belgian pilots were trained at the French flying school at Étampes, south of Paris. In addition, a number were trained in the UK and de Trixhe was one of these.

Born on 19 October 1896 at Sprimont, Liège, he joined the *6me Regiment d'Artillerie* on 2 August 1914. Just over a year later, in

Baron Fernand de Woot de Trixhe. Note the RFC wings above his left pocket.

September 1915, he transferred to the air service and undertook his initial training with the Military School at Hendon and earned his Royal Aero Club certificate, No. 2076, on 21 November 1915, flying a Maurice Farman biplane.

He was posted to 1*ère Escadrille*, based at Les Moëres (page 90), commanded by *Capitaine* Fernand Jacquet, in January 1917. His first non-operational flight was on the 26th of that month with his commanding officer. King Albert was very supportive of the *Aviation Militaire Belge* and on 18 March 1917 he flew over the lines with Jacquet, while De Trixhe flew a protection patrol. It is interesting to speculate what the Germans would have made of King Albert if he had been forced to land behind their lines!

Unfortunately on 31 May De Trixhe was killed when his Nieuport scout crashed on the aerodrome at Les Moëres. In his short four month career he had flown 59 patrols and had two inconclusive aerial combats. He was buried the following day. His awards include being made a *Chevalier de l'Ordre de Leopold II*, the *Croix de Guerre* and the *Médaille de l'Yser.*

In his autobiography *Days on the Wing (Jours Envolés)*, Willy Coppens, Belgium's greatest fighter ace, wrote:

> *On May 29* (sic), *we lost Fernand de Woote de Trixhe, another excellent fellow, who had been transferred to the 1st Single-Seater Fighter Squadron. Actually, de Trixhe would have been better employed in a two-seater squadron. He met his death as a result of stalling his Nieuport after losing his engine while taking off, a mistake he would scarcely have made in a machine not quite so capricious as the Baby Nieuport.*

Paul Charles Gustave Hanciau (743)

The second grave we are visiting is just three to the left of de Trixhe's.

Hanciau was born on 26 January 1885 at Ixelles, Brussels. Quite old by First World War flying standards he was a pre-war pilot, having received brevet No. 34 on 23 February 1911. On 6 August 1914 a machine was donated to the *Aviation Militaire Belge* by the *Societé des Aviateurs Belges* and Hanciau was chosen to fly it but, unfortunately, he crashed-landed it only eight days later. In May 1915 he was assigned to the aviation service full time and six months later flew his first patrols, then being posted to the 1ère *Escadrille* at the end of January 1916. During 1916 he flew 64 patrols and forced three enemy machines back to their lines.

By 30 September 1917 Hanciau had flown a total of 156 patrols and had been involved in six combats, without a decisive conclusion. On this day he left for an afternoon mission flying a Nieuport 23 in company with *Adjutant* Goossens-Bara. Hanciau was attacked by ten Albatros scouts, who caught him by surprise and wounded him in the

Hanciau in front of his Nieuport Scout. All his machines carried the name *Soit*! (Let It Be).

carotid artery. Turning for the Belgian lines he attempted an emergency landing near some Belgian troops, but at a low altitude, suddenly dived into the ground and was killed.

He was made a *Chevalier de l'Ordre de Leopold* and, as well as the *Croix de Guerre*, was awarded four *Chevrons de front*.

Willy Coppens again:

> *Hanciau was a pre-war pilot, a capable fellow and a very good sort. His wife had followed him to the front, where she lived in one of the farms near our huts. This did not affect Hanciau's ambition to shoot down his first German machine. The patrol had not been gone an hour when a telephone message informed us that one of our machines had been shot down in the course of a flight. Which of the two was it? The other would have to continue his patrol, and we did not know which of the two had been killed, a fact that added to the tragedy of the thing. At last, after another hour had gone by, we saw one of our machines coming back, and watched it turn and land. Then, unable to restrain ourselves, we rushed forward to meet it, to find out for ourselves, and recognised Goossens sitting in the cockpit.*

> *We buried Hanciau, where many others of our number had been buried, in the little cemetery at Adinkerque, and the carpenters of the squadron made him a cross of propeller-wood.*

The Belgian craftsman possesses that signal quality of pride in his work, and of artistry in its execution.

One day, Olieslagers chanced to go into the workshop and saw one of these crosses of propeller-walnut standing in a corner, beautifully polished. We had not lost a pilot for some considerable time, and he was not a little surprised. 'Whom is this cross for?' he asked; and the carpenter replied, simply: 'The next.'

The Sopwith Camel

In the front row of this cemetery is a single line of CWGC graves containing RNAS personnel. However, the burial we have come specifically to see is at the very back of the burial ground on the right hand side. The grave of Flight Sub Lieutenant Eric William Busby is in the centre of the nearer of the two rows of War Graves Commission headstones.

If asked what was the most famous First World War fighter, I suspect that most of the general public would reply that it was the Sopwith Camel. There were more claims made by pilots flying this machine than any other.

In the spring of 1917 the British flying services were at a great disadvantage in that the Germans had equipped with more modern machines but the RFC were still awaiting new types. Consequently, during the Battle of Arras, they suffered such horrendous casualties that the period was later called 'Bloody April'. What modern machines they had, such as the Bristol Fighter and SE5, were only available in small numbers.

During December 1916 the experimental department of the Sopwith Company passed the design of a new machine designated the F1, powered by the 110 hp Clerget 9Z. It had a deeper fuselage than the Pup and with its engine, guns, pilot and fuel concentrated near the front this gave it a hunched appearance, hence the nickname of Camel. The compact arrangement, together with the torque of the rotary engine, gave the Camel excellent manoeuvrability. In addition it mounted two Vickers machine guns compared to the Pup's one.

Two prototypes were quickly acquired by the Admiralty, of which one was sent to France for evaluation. The navy were not slow in ordering the new machine and the first production aeroplane arrived at Dunkirk on 15 May 1917. The first unit to receive Camels was 4 Naval Squadron based at Bray-Dunes (page 99), with the initial machine arriving on 26 May. Within a week they had completely re-equipped with it. The first confirmed victories occurred on 5 June when Flight

Commander A M Shook of 4 Naval brought down two machines between Nieuport and Ostend. The first machine lost on active service was N6362 on 13 June 1917 (page 46).

The first loss to enemy action was on 17 July when E W Busby of 4 Naval failed to return.

Eric William Busby

Born on 27 November 1897 Busby came from Birmingham. He joined the RNAS in July 1916 and trained at Crystal Palace, Chingford and Cranwell. Gaining his Royal Aeronautical Certificate, number 3996, at Chingford on 10 December 1916 he was posted to Dover on 14 April 1917. By the end of June 1917 he had a total of eighty flying hours.

On 10 July information was received from the RFC that enemy machines were out in force to the west of Nieuport. As a consequence 4 Naval's patrol was increased to five machines, and this lifted off from Bray-Dunes at 1930 hours. The leader was an experienced Canadian, acting Flight Commander Arnold Jacques Chadwick, who had claimed a number of victories. At 13,000 feet over Coxyde the patrol attacked three twin-engined machines, which were being fired upon by Allied anti-aircraft guns. The enemy machines were joined by a formation of ten Albatros scouts. In the ensuing fight Chadwick claimed two of the scouts brought down out of control but Busby was seen to be attacked by four enemy aeroplanes over Pervyse, southeast of Nieuport, and then go down with a wing missing. He was killed and the remains of his machine were retrieved, then returned to the Aircraft Depot. Chadwick was shot down and killed a few days later on 28 July and is buried in Adinkerke Military Cemetery next to F D Casey (see page 104).

E W Busby, the pilot of the first Sopwith Camel lost to enemy action.

Georg Strasser

Busby's likely victor would appear to be Georg Strasser of *Jasta* 17. He had joined them on 11 November 1916 when they were stationed down on the French front. Quickly getting into his stride, Strasser brought down his first machine, a Caudron, on Boxing Day 1916,

Georg Strasser and his Albatros DV of *Jasta* 17.

northwest of Fort Douaumont. On 24 June 1917 the unit was moved north to Ghistelles, near Ostend, to reinforce the German air service in the face of the British offensive at Ypres. Busby was his fourth victory and after claiming his seventh he was transferred to a training unit in May 1918. He died on 4 December 1925.

Return to the main road by the church, and turn left. Continue through Adinkerke, and look for a large water tower on the left hand side of the road. Opposite the water tower is the entrance to the cemetery, marked by the small Belgian signs. Turn right, taking care crossing the tram tracks, and continue through the civilian cemetery to the military plot beyond.

De Panne Belgian Cemetery

There are 3,876 burials here and this includes several Belgian air service personnel casualties. The grave we have come to visit is situated in the second block on the right before the island and is in the centre of the front row.

The other *AMB* flying casualties are:

William Cornesse (B222). Killed in a flying accident, 21 May 1918.
Didier Malherbe (C193). Killed in a flying accident, 4 June 1918.
Victor van Stappen (C202). Killed in a flying accident, 19 May 1918.
Richard E Fanning (C241). Killed by a shell splinter, 7 April 1917.
Jean Demot (F244). Killed by a shell, 5 October 1918 with Eckstein.

Serge Eckstein (F245). Killed by a shell, 5 October 1918, with Demot.

Jean de Roest d'Alkemade (F247). Shot down and killed, 28 September 1918.

Jules Arthur Joseph Dony (G228). Killed in a flying accident, 1 October 1918.

Max Roland (G233). Shot down and killed, 3 October 1918, with Gisseleire.

Albert Gisseleire (G234). Shot down and killed, 3 October 1918, with Roland.

Capitaine-Commandant **Jules Arthur Joseph Dony** (G228)

Dony was born in Ixelles, Brussels on 3 April 1890. A pre-war regular soldier, he enlisted in December 1908 and was commissioned in March 1911. He had an early interest in flying and obtained his brevet, No. 74, in June 1913 and became a military aviator four months later when he joined the *Compagnie des Aviateurs*. Just a month before, in September 1913, Dony was made a *Chevalier de l'Ordre de la Couronne*. Though he was a pilot, in the early days of the war he flew as an observer with the French unit *MS*26 (the *MS* designator indicating they were flying Morane-Saulnier machines). In October he was transferred to the *AMB*. Initially he flew observation machines but at the end of 1915 commenced flying offensive patrols. Unfortunately this did not last long as on Boxing Day he crashed his Nieuport following engine failure and received facial injuries.

Two months later he joined the *5me Escadrille* and in August, when the *5me Escadrille de Chasse* was formed, he was given command of it. Like many RFC commanding officers Dony did not fly a great deal but nonetheless was a good CO.

He remained in command of the unit until his death on 1 October 1918. In the morning he had attacked two enemy machines on the ground at an aerodrome near Roulers but while taking off for his second patrol he crashed his Spad and was killed. Despite not flying a lot Dony had participated in a third of the *Group*

114

Capitaine-Commandant **Dony, commanding the** *Escadrille de Chasse.*

de Chasse patrols and been involved in seven combats, though he was not credited with any victories. He had been made a *Chevalier de l'Ordre de Leopold* and awarded the *Croix de Guerre*. From the French he received the *Croix de Guerre* and was made a *Chevalier de l'Ordre de la Légion d'Honneur* and from the Russians the Order of St Stanilaus 3rd Class.

Willy Coppens wrote of him:

> *On October 1st we lost Commandant Donis* (sic), *whose Spad crashed near our quarters. His engine had cut out, and he lost flying-speed while trying to extend his glide to miss a ditch. The machine fell vertically, head downwards, and struck the ground with tremendous force. Donis was killed instantaneously. He was such a popular figure in our Flying Corps that we were overwhelmed, especially his pilots and men. One of the mechanics of his squadron wept openly.*

Drive back over the tram tracks, and at the main road turn right. Continue into De Panne, and turn right for Centrum, then at the traffic lights right again on the E40 Veurne. Turn left onto the N396 Koksijde as the road goes to the right, then at the roundabout go straight ahead on the N396 Nieuwpoort. Continue ahead to the cemetery on the left side of road. The cemetery is set some distance back from the road down a well manicured grass path.

Coxyde Military Cemetery

In June 1917 British forces relieved French units on a six kilometre front from the sea to a point just south of Nieuport for a six month period. The area was sufficiently behind the front line to be used as rest billets and suffered only occasional shelling. This cemetery (No. 41) had been started by the French and after the British withdrawal in December 1917 continued to be used by them. After the Armistice further casualties were brought in from the battlefield and other cemeteries. In addition further burials were made after the Dunkirk operations of 1940. The cemetery now contains over 1,500 graves from the Great War and 154 from the Second World War. The French graves have since been removed.

There are a number of interesting burials here and the first results from a disastrous day for 213 Squadron RAF. From the entrance proceed to the left and in the second row from the front we are paying our respects to the casualty nine graves from the right.

John Edmund Greene (II K9)

Greene, a Canadian from Winnipeg, Manitoba, was born on 2 July 1894 and attended the University of Manitoba from October 1915 to May 1916. He was recruited directly in Canada by the RNAS and gained his Royal Aero Club certificate, No. 4060, on 19 December 1916 at the Curtiss School in Toronto. After training at Crystal Palace and Vendôme, south of Paris, he was commissioned as a flight sub-lieutenant. Posted to Dunkirk in October he was then sent to the Seaplane Defence Squadron at St. Pol (page 150). On 4 December 1917 he drove down a kite balloon from which the observer took to his parachute. On 15 January 1918 the Seaplane Defence Squadron reformed as Number 13 Naval Squadron and was equipped with Sopwith Camels. On 29 January Greene claimed his first official victory when he shot down a seaplane off the Belgian coast.

J E Greene killed on 14 October 1918, barely one month before the war ended.

On 1 April 1918 the RNAS and RFC merged to become the Royal Air Force and 13 Naval became 213 Squadron. The same day Greene claimed another seaplane as his fourth victim. By 8 October he had claimed fourteen victories and had been awarded the DFC.

The 14 October began with a patrol at 0930 hours by nineteen Camels against retreating German troops, during which Greene and Kenneth MacLeish claimed a Fokker DVII. As a result of heavy opposition three 213 machines failed to return. Two hours after the first patrol returned fifteen aeroplanes left on another operation and two miles north of Dixmude the formation encountered eleven Fokker DVIIs at 8,000 feet, with another three at 12,000 feet. A number of enemy machines were claimed but two Camels were seen to go down in flames. On landing back at Bergues three Camels were found to be missing, Greene, F R L Allen and Kenneth MacLeish. Greene's body was found at Pervyse.

Allen's remains were never found and his name appears on the Air Forces Memorial to the Missing at Arras. In June 1919 his mother wrote to the officer commanding 213 Squadron, asking for news of him and in her letter she quoted a piece from one of her son's letters:

> *The CO is a jolly decent sport and really one wouldn't think he was a major to see him acting the goat with us. Now you know that sort of man deserves all the loyal support he can get and certainly does get mine.*

Allen's mother concluded her letter:

> *Now will you please enquire of the Major (I am sorry I do not know his name) for I would like to thank him for giving my boy a good time.*

The major referred to was Ronald Graham who, for his services during the First World War, received the DSO, DSC and Bar and the DFC. He was a very active commanding officer and was involved in an amusing incident described by David Ingalls, an American pilot, in a letter home:

> *Amusing things do happen, even in war. On another raid the C.O. was chasing a poor bloke who was legging it on a bicycle for dear life. Pretty soon this German blighter hopped off the road and ducked behind a stone wall to hide like a rabbit. When the C.O. banked around to see where his quarry had gone, the fellow up and heaved a brick at him. It smashed a tremendous hole in the wing of the plane. Imagine a man stoning an aeroplane!*

Graham retired from the RAF in 1948 as an Air Vice-Marshal, having also been awarded the CB and CBE. He died in Scotland on 23 June 1967.

Kenneth MacLeish

Ken was born on 19 September 1894 at Glencoe, Illinois, a suburb north of Chicago on the shore of Lake Michigan. One of four children (his elder brother Archibald became one of America's most renowned poets) Kenneth entered Yale University in the autumn of 1914. An excellent athlete, he joined the First Yale Unit, a privately sponsored organization established to produce aviators. In March 1917 the Yale aviators were persuaded to join the Naval Reserve Flying Corps. Flying training began at West Palm Beach, Florida and on 2 May MacLeish went solo. After some instructing he sailed for Europe in late October 1917.

Leutnant zur See Reinhold Poss in his Albatros DVa. He commanded 1 *Seefrontstaffel* from May until September 1918, when he took command of *MFJ*IV. He claimed two Camels on 14 October 1918. After eleven victories he was shot down and taken prisoner on 15 October 1918. He was killed when flying into a church steeple on 26 August 1933.

In March 1918 he was posted to Dunkirk to fly seaplanes, just in time for the great German spring offensive and, due to the shortage of pilots, MacLeish, David Ingalls (page 61) and another pilot were temporarily assigned to 13 Naval. However after three weeks they returned to flying their seaplanes. In June and July MacLeish spent some time attached to 218 Squadron flying DH9s before temporary duty with headquarters US Naval Air Service in Paris. He was able to return to front line service, arriving at Dunkirk on the evening of 13 October 1918, for further duty

Vizeflugmeister **Karl Scharon, third from the right. Flying with** *Marinefeldjasta* **II he was credited with eight victories and was awarded the Iron Cross First Class. He died on 26 May 1921.**

Pilots of *MFJ*II in front of a Pfalz DIII. Standing on the left is *Vizeflugmeister* Alexandre Zenses, *Marinefeldjasta* II. By the end of the war he had claimed nineteen victories and been awarded the Iron Cross Second Class.

Flugmeister Gerhard Hubrich (left) and his mechanics. Born on 30 July 1896 *Kuken* (Chicken) qualified as a pilot in October 1914. A reconnaissance pilot, he joined *Seefrontstaffel* in 1918, which became *Marinefeldjasta* IV. He claimed twelve victories. In the Second World War he served as a major and died on 20 October 1972.

with 213 Squadron. The following day he carried out one short test flight and then went missing on his second patrol.

MacLeish's body was not found until Boxing Day, over two months after his loss. A Mr Alfred Rouse, returning to his farm, twelve kilometres southwest of Ostend, to investigate the damage, found Kenneth's remains behind the stables, approximately 200 yards from the wreckage of his machine. The body was in an advanced state of decomposition but there were enough documents to identify the remains. It would seem he fell from his aeroplane before it hit the ground. He was buried where he was found but later removed to the US cemetery at Wareghem (*Ypres* page 151) and is buried in grave B.4.1. MacLeish's letters were published in 1991 as *The Price of Honor*.

Because of the scale of activity at the end of the war and lack of records it is difficult to establish who claimed 213's casualties, though it was almost certainly pilots from the German marine units in Flanders. Gerhard Hubrich, Reinhold Poss, Karl Scharon and Alexandre Zenses brought down five Camels on 14 October 1918.

Sadly, of the six Camels lost by 213 Squadron, only one pilot survived as a prisoner and of the other five two have no known grave.

Charles Robert Reeves Hickey (II K12)

Three graves along the row from J E Greene is another decorated naval fighter pilot, C R R Hickey. His case demonstrates that to survive and be successful you not only need skill but a large slice of luck as well.

Hickey was born in Nanaimo, British Columbia, on 10 September 1897. His father was a major in the 11th Canadian Mounted Rifles which Charles also joined as a private after the outbreak of war. In February 1917 he joined the RNAS and completed his flying training at Vendôme and Dunkirk, following which he was posted to 4 Naval at Bray-Dunes on 30 July 1917. They had recently become the first unit to be completely equipped with the new Sopwith Camel. Three weeks after his arrival Hickey claimed his first enemy machine, an Albatros DV out of control southeast of Ostend. On 21 April 1918 he

C R R Hickey.

brought down a Rumpler two-seater on the Allied side of the lines and landed near to it. While attempting to keep Belgian civilians away from it the machine exploded and he received burns to the face and hands. Hickey was admitted to the Queen Alexandra Hospital at Dunkirk and was discharged on 4 May. In August his DFC was gazetted, by which time he had shot down nine enemy machines and shortly afterwards he was promoted to acting flight commander. The following month a Bar to his DFC was announced. On 1 October he made his last claim, having accounted for twenty-one hostile aircraft.

At 1520 hours on 3 October 1918, in company with twenty-one other Camels, Hickey left on an Offensive Patrol in the Nieuport – Thourout - Roulers area. It was cloudy over the lines and ground visibility was poor. No enemy aircraft were seen but shortly after diving through cloud Hickey collided with Lieutenant S E Matthey, another member of the patrol, at 12,000 feet over Ramscappelle and was killed.

Schomberg Edward Matthey (II K11)

Matthey, who is buried in the next grave to Hickey, must have been one of the youngest pilots in the RAF during the Great War. He was born on 2 February 1900 and when he joined the RNAS on 24 February 1918 was only three weeks past his eighteenth birthday. From January 1913 until August 1917 he had been a student at Cheltenham College, where he served as a private in the OTC. After training he arrived at No. 5 Pilot's Pool and was posted to 204 Squadron (as it had become on 1 April 1918 with the formation of the RAF) on 16 September. He was killed just over two weeks later, still aged only eighteen.

A Captured Gotha (A4)

Just on the left side of the cemetery is a small German plot and here we find a member of the so-called 'England Squadron', *Leutnant der Reserve* Alfred Herzberg, who were so successful in bombing the United Kingdom during 1917 (page 69).

A Gotha had fallen into British hands on the Western Front on 23 April 1917 when Flight Lieutenant Lloyd Breadner, flying a Sopwith Pup of 3 Naval, brought one down. This was comprehensively analysed by intelligence and given the captured aircraft number G23. The crew survived as prisoners and were interrogated.

During the night of 25 September anti-aircraft fire in the Fourth Army area brought another example down, near Dunkirk, from the same unit, *Staffel* 15 of *Kagohl III*. The gunner, *Vizefeldwebel* Wilhelm Wienecke, survived as a prisoner, though wounded, but the pilot, *Leutnant* Alfred Herzberg, and the observer, *Leutnant* Franz Rahning, were both killed. At some later date Rahning's remains must have been returned to Germany.

Part of the undercarriage of G74.

Though recognised as the same type as G23, Herzberg's machine, which was allocated the number G74, was also very carefully inspected to see if there had been any improvements or alterations. The technical report consisted of five pages, though the Gotha was little more than a collection of pieces. In fact only the top of the fuselage remained, as the rest had been destroyed by fire. It was noted that the dope on the fabric covering was of very poor quality. Much interest

The remains of the fuselage of G74, showing the gunner's weapon pointing down the underside tunnel. The wire guards were to prevent him putting his hands into the propellers. In the background the wings can be seen laid out on the ground.

centred round ancillary fittings, and the oxygen set, air speed indicator, part of the bomb sight apparatus, battery and petrol cocks were sent to the Air Board in London for further investigation. The petrol cocks were described as *of rather neat design*.

Return to the roundabout on the N396, and turn left onto the N8 Veurne. Pass the end of the runway of the present day airfield on the left, then turn right for Ten Bogaerde, the large farm complex set back from the road.

Furnes/Coxyde Aerodrome

With the fall of Antwerp, four of the five Belgian *escadrilles* moved to Ostend on 4 October 1914. A week later all five evacuated to St-Pol-sur-Mer but on the 17th I *Escadrille* moved forward to the aerodrome at Coxyde (or Furnes as it was known to the British). They were shortly joined by *Escadrilles* II and III. Initial equipment consisted of a mixture of Maurice Farmans and Voisin pushers. Being so close to the front line, the aerodrome was a target for the batteries of heavy guns established by the Germans along the North Sea coast.

The aerodrome was used by A Squadron of No.1 Wing RNAS from June 1916 for the defence of Dunkirk and it was from here that Roderick Dallas (*Arras* page 115), the great Australian ace, scored a number of his victories. On 6 December 1916 the Detached Flight (as A Squadron had been re-designated) became No. 1 (Naval) Squadron.

Picture No.15. Furnes aerodrome looking southeast in 2004.

Furnes/Coxyde Aerodrome

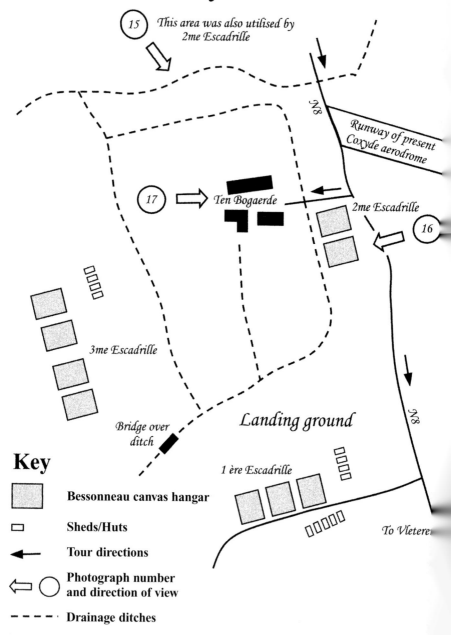

15 *This area was also utilised by 2me Escadrille*

N8

Runway of present Coxyde aerodrome

17 → *Ten Bogaerde*

2me Escadrille

16

3me Escadrille

N8

Landing ground

Bridge over ditch

1 ère Escadrille

To Vleteren

Key

Bessonneau canvas hangar

Sheds/Huts

Tour directions

Photograph number and direction of view

- - - - Drainage ditches

Picture No.16. Furnes on 24 July 1916 during the ceremony in which Roderick Dallas was presented with his *Croix de Guerre*.

Their stay at Furnes ended in February 1917 when they moved out to reinforce the RFC on the Somme. Other naval units stationed here were 3 Naval, 8 Naval, 9 Naval and 10 Naval, all of which were fighter squadrons. The last RNAS unit to be based here was 3 Naval, which departed on 6 September 1917, and the aerodrome was not used again.

Two notable events occurred at this spot. The first was on 7 June 1915 when Rex Warneford of 1 Wing RNAS took off and shot down the German airship *LZ37*, thus earning the Victoria Cross (page 25). The second was when J A Liddell landed here on 31 July 1915 badly wounded after his Victoria Cross action (page 164).

Drive back to the road and turn right. Continue along the N8 to Vleteren and turn right N321 Westvleteren. After the entering Westvleteren sign, take the next left turn into St. Maartens Straat. Continue through the housing estate to the cemetery.

Picture No.17. View past the farm to the road with the hangars on the right.

Westvleteren Belgian Cemetery

The cemetery contains 1,100 Belgian casualties and one Briton. The grave we have come to visit is in the front row on the left as you enter and is the second one along from the right hand end.

This casualty, Robert Deprost, was the only Belgian kite balloon observer to be shot down and killed during the Great War. Born on 12 May 1893 in Avelgem he was an engineer before joining up. He enlisted on 14 July 1915 and late the next year was posted to III*me Section Aéronautique*. They had only been operational since 25 August. Deprost's first ascent was on 15 September 1916 and his companion was Jean Demot, who was to be killed himself by a shell on 5 October 1918. Deprost's career was destined to be very short because on Sunday, 1 October, while ranging an artillery battery, his balloon was shot down. It was believed he left parachuting out too late and the burning fabric fell upon him. In common with all other Belgian soldiers killed he was made a *Chevalier de l'Ordre de Léopold II* and awarded the *Croix de Guerre*.

Robert Deprost.

He was the first victory of *Vizefeldwebel* Alfred Ulmer of *Jasta* 8. Though Ulmer only claimed five victories, three of them feature in the *Airfields and Airmen* series. The

Jasta 8 in April 1917. Front row fourth from the left is Walter Göttsch (page 39). Seventh from the left is Alfred Ulmer. Second from the left in the back row is Hans von Hünerbein (*Cambrai* page 71).

reader will remember that he brought down C A Felix-Brown and J W W Nason of 46 Squadron on 26 December 1916 as his third victory. He also shot down Sergeant C S Tooms of 41 Squadron on 24 January 1917 as his fifth and last victory. Both events appear in *Ypres* page 32.

Alfred Ulmer and the *Ehrenbecher*

Ulmer was born on 15 September 1896 in Reutlingen, south of Stuttgart. He was posted to *Jasta* 8 as a *vizefeldwebel* on 10 September 1916 and just over three weeks later claimed his first victory.

For a first victory every member of the *Fliegertruppe* or German air service was eligible for a silver cup, which was sponsored by rich industrialists. This was only awarded for the first victory and as the war progressed and silver became scarce they were eventually manufactured from iron. It is possible that it was not awarded to everyone and later in the war eight to nine victories were needed to qualify for it. Around the base is the inscription *Dem Sieger im Luftkampf* or Victor in Air Combat. They were usually presented on a base and in a case, though these tend to be lost.

On 5 February 1917 Ulmer was severely wounded in a fight with a Nieuport two-seater of 46 Squadron. He returned to *Jasta* 8 but made no further claims before being killed on 29 June 1917. Attacking an FE2 of 20 Squadron flown by Lieutenant Harold Waddell Joslyn and his observer Private E A Potter he was shot down in flames. Joslyn, a Canadian from Saskatchewan, who was born on 9 October 1893, joined 20 Squadron on 30 May 1917. Over the next three months he and his gunners claimed seven enemy scout machines (five with Potter). On 17 August he was shot down and killed, probably by pilots from *Jasta* 6 or 26. Neither he nor his observer, Lieutenant Alexander Urquhart, have a known grave and are commemorated on the Air Services Memorial to the Missing at Arras.

The *Ehrenbecher* (Cup of Honour). This particular one was given to Anton Bauhofer, who claimed four victories with *Jasta* 25 in Macedonia.

The certificate that accompanied an *Ehrenbeche*r. Maximilian Edler von Daniels, after service with *Jastas* 15, 23 and 83, was killed on 7 June 1918 while serving with *Jasta* 61.

Return to the main road, and turn left through the village, then right for Krombeke. In Krombeke turn left for Poperinge. The country becomes more wooded, and look for a wood on the left hand side of the road. The cemetery is in this wood down a (sometimes) muddy track to the left, opposite a green **CWGC** sign.

Dozinghem Military Cemetery

Westvleteren was not part of the British sphere of operations but in July 1917, in anticipation of the Third Battle of Ypres, three casualty clearing stations were established here, the 4th, 47th and 61st. This cemetery (No. 44) was employed by them until early 1918. There are now 3,174 Commonwealth burials, plus another seventy-three from the Dunkirk evacuation of May 1940. In addition there are sixty-five German war graves from the First World War. At one time there were some Belgian graves in front of the Cross of Sacrifice but this area now contains the Second World War casualties.

George Leonard Trapp (XIV G14)

The grave we have come to visit is situated at the rear of the cemetery, just to the left of the Stone of Remembrance in the third row from the front and nearest the central aisle.

This casualty is particularly sad as Trapp was one of three brothers who were all killed in the flying services during the First World War.

George was the middle brother and was born on 1 July 1894 to Thomas John and Nellie Kathleen Trapp of New Westminster, British Columbia. He joined the RNAS on 19 January 1917 and graduated as a flight sub-lieutenant on 14 June. Initially he served with 12 Naval but on 14 July 1917 was posted to 10 Naval, who were flying Sopwith Triplanes from Droglandt (page 192). Just a month later he claimed his first enemy machine, when he sent an Albatros DIII out of control. Three victories were claimed flying the Triplane before the squadron exchanged them in July for Sopwith Camels. He claimed another three enemy machines, the last being on the

George Leonard Trapp

Camel B3882 of 10 Naval. George Trapp claimed two victories in this machine. It also served with 6 Naval and 12 Naval but was destroyed in a fatal accident.

morning of 12 November 1917, when he destroyed a two-seater. At 1510 hours on the same day he took off, leading a patrol of eight Camels to patrol near Dixmude. Observing an enemy observation machine at 6,000 feet, they dived on it. Trapp's machine was seen to break up in the air and the wreckage fell in to the Allied lines. No other German machines were seen and the two-seater made its escape.

There has been some confusion concerning Trapp's loss and indeed the date of his death is incorrectly shown in Commonwealth War Graves Commission records as 13 November. In one publication he has been credited to *Oberleutnant* Bruno Justinius of *Jasta* 35b but his Camel claim was for the day following Trapp's death. Whether the gunner of the German two-seater had a lucky hit on the Camel or it suffered structural failure is impossible to establish.

Another of 10 Naval's pilots was the great Canadian ace Raymond Collishaw, who wrote in his autobiography *Air Command*:

> *Amongst the many families that I visited during my leave was that of George Trapp, who had flown with me on Naval Ten. The family lived in New Westminster, B.C., near Vancouver, and Mr Trapp was a well-known resident, highly-respected for his charitable work and community activities. Three sons had joined the British flying services. Stanley, like his brother George, had joined the RNAS and had been killed in December 1916 while flying with No. 8 (Naval) Squadron. The third, Donovan, had become an RFC pilot. None was to survive the war. George was killed with Naval Ten during my Canadian leave and Donovan was killed in 1918 while flying with No. 85 Squadron. While visiting the family I met the two sisters, both lovely girls, and I*

129

was immediately much taken by one of them, Neita. I returned to
New Westminster during my leave and before I left for overseas
we had become engaged. It was, though, almost six years before
we were able to marry.

For a fuller account of Collishaw's career see page 194.

Stanley Valentine Trapp

Born on 14 February 1890 he was the
eldest son. Learning to fly at Chingford and
Cranwell, he gained his 'ticket', No. 2493, on 12
February 1916, and was posted to Dover on 18
May 1916. He joined 8 Naval, who were based at
Vert Galand and had been loaned to the RFC
during the Battle of the Somme.

Geoffrey Bromet, commanding 8 Naval
(later Air Vice-Marshal Sir Geoffrey KBE,
CB, DSO) wrote:

> *On December 10th we had a*
> *very bad crash on the aerodrome,*
> *resulting in the death of Trapp. He had*
> *his 'Sopwith' up for a test flight and, on*   **Stanley Valentine Trapp.**
> *pulling out of a very steep dive, the*
> *machine folded up. He was a splendid type of Canadian whom*
> *everybody liked, and he was an exceptionally courageous and*
> *brilliant fighting pilot.*

The machine broke up at 150 feet and was totally destroyed in the crash
and subsequent fire. Trapp was buried the following day at Beauval
Communal Cemetery (No. 417) in grave A19.

Donovan Joseph Trapp

Donovan was the youngest brother, born on 23 November 1896. He
was a student at New Westminster High School from 1912 until 1915.
Joining the RFC at South Farnborough, he learned to fly at 24 Training
Squadron and the Central Flying School. He was posted to 85
Squadron and went with them to France the following day. The unit
flew to Marquise and then Petite-Synthe, before settling at St. Omer
(page 158), their base for the next two months.

On 19 July 1918 Trapp left on a patrol at 1700 hours and was last
seen over enemy lines. He probably fell victim to *Unteroffizier* Marat
Schumm of *Jasta* 52, who claimed an SE5a at 1845 hours north of
Estaires. Trapp's name is recorded on one of a number of special

memorials in Anzac Cemetery at Sailly-sur-la-Lys, south east of Armentières. These remember casualties whose exact grave location within the cemetery have been lost.

Return down the track to the main road and turn left. Shortly after the yellow Poperinge sign, La Lovie Chateau is visible through the trees on the right-hand side of the road. Opposite the end of the wood on the right is a metalled track to the left marked with a 'Dead End' sign. Turn left into the track and park.

La Lovie Aerodrome

This aerodrome first became operational in May 1917 when 21 Squadron arrived in anticipation of the commencement of Haig's Flanders offensive with the Battle of Messines on 7 June. They were joined by 23 Squadron the following month. Other units based here at various times were 29, 35, 65 and 74 Squadrons.

Adjacent to the aerodrome is the chateau at La Lovie, which is now a medical institution. In his autobiography, *Air of Battle*, W M Fry, a flight commander in 23 Squadron, wrote:

> *The lodge gates to La Lovie Chateau were just across the road from our mess, and General Gough and members of his 5th Army Staff, being mostly cavalrymen and long-standing friends of our CO, were frequently in our mess. When the general came to luncheon or dinner, he was obviously intrigued by the mixture of young pilots from different countries and no two uniforms alike.*

Picture No.18. La Lovie looking south in 2005.

La Lovie Aerodrome

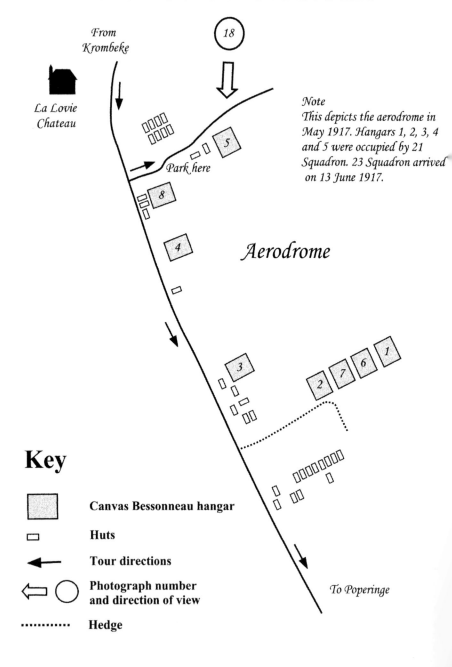

From Krombeke

18

La Lovie Chateau

Park here

5

8

4

Aerodrome

Note
This depicts the aerodrome in May 1917. Hangars 1, 2, 3, 4 and 5 were occupied by 21 Squadron. 23 Squadron arrived on 13 June 1917.

3

2 7 6 1

To Poperinge

Key

Canvas Bessonneau hangar

Huts

Tour directions

Photograph number and direction of view

Hedge

Everything about us must have been strange to a correct cavalry soldier, but he was so friendly and charming that we all loved him at first sight. As soon as he entered our mess he threw off all rank, and for the time it was hard to realise that he was the Army commander responsible for the conduct of the Passchendaele battle then in progress.

Like a lot of aerodromes hurriedly brought into use during the First World War, La Lovie's position was less than ideal, with a hop field containing tall poles on its eastern boundary.

Guy Burgess, an RE8 pilot in 21 Squadron, wrote:

My first flight with 21 Squadron in France was a shocker, I had not been briefed in any way as to the state of the airfield, which in Jany (sic) was pretty soft, so proceeded to take off, with the usual sand bags as passenger, taking as long a run as possible. By the time I was nearly 'out of airfield' I was barely airborne, through the muddy conditions, and had no chance of clearing the trees at the end of the airfield so just took the best course possible between 2 trees, shedding my wings on impact, the fuselage with me intact, went along merrily. I was out of the wreck in seconds, fearing fire. I was only badly shaken, and within a matter of minutes, was safely airborne in another machine. Incidentally this was the only time I damaged an aircraft throughout my service in France, which consisted of 346 hours, so can consider myself one of the lucky ones.

Burgess later flew with 7 Squadron, also flying the RE8 on corps duties, and spent eight months on operational flying.

RE8 B5075 'J' of 21 Squadron, showing their dumb-bell marking.

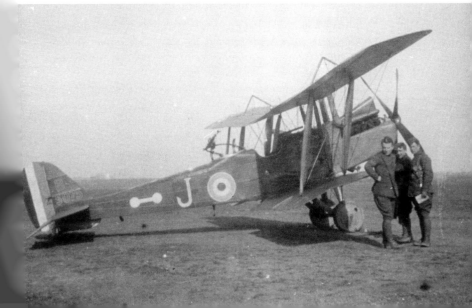

Spad Type XIII B6389 of 23 Squadron. This served with the unit from 29 December 1917 until crashed on 9 March 1918. Note the rounded wingtips, which distinguish it from the Type VII.

The Spad 13

In *Airfields and Airmen: Arras* page 73, the French Spad 7 was described in relation to 19 Squadron and its commanding officer, Major H D Harvey-Kelly. Only two RFC squadrons were fully equipped with the type, though it served in great numbers with the French, Italian, Belgian and US air services. The type 7 was redesigned as the type 13 with two Vickers machine guns and a 200 hp geared Hispano-Suiza engine which gave it a much improved performance. However, due to problems with its engine, production was slow.

The RFC converted part of its Spad 7 order into type 13s but, owing to shortage of materials and the fact some of its order was directed to the French, deliveries were late, with only sixty being delivered by the end of March 1918. As a consequence 23 Squadron became the only RFC unit to be completely equipped with it. Willie Fry wrote of the Spad:

> It was a beautifully built aeroplane, very strong, which made it rather heavy, and it was reputed to have the gliding angle of a brick, with the engine throttled back or shut off. For this reason it was not popular with some RFC pilots.
>
> The SPAD was comfortable to sit in, with a roomy seat and plenty of elbow room on each side, and with a well-padded cockpit fairing at precisely the right height to enable one to look over the side downwards behind the trailing edge of the bottom wings. The all-round view downward was not very good, but somehow the view behind the bottom wings afforded an excellent field for picking up machines flying below, and a slight turn either way increased the field of view tremendously. It was a bit of a

134

hazard that the pilot's seat was the petrol tank specially adapted and shaped for this purpose, with a wicker seat and cushion on top. A few bullets through the tank, especially if there were a tracer or two amongst them, betokened the end in those days of no parachutes and forty or more gallons beneath one's bottom.

About this time we began to be issued with, as replacements, an improved type of SPAD with a more powerful Hispano engine, a 220-h.p instead of the previous 180-h.p, and a geared drive to the propeller instead of direct off the crankshaft. These new machines also had two Vickers guns between the cylinder blocks under the cowling, both firing through the propeller, the guns being speeded up in some way and firing much faster than the standard ground-type of Vickers; a tremendous improvement on the one gun.

These new aeroplanes were much superior to the old type, except the geared drive in the engines was unreliable and had a tendency to strip. We missed the comforting roar of the old direct-drive engine, the geared one being rather noisy and rough.

Despite the improved machine, 23 Squadron achieved no great successes with it and in April 1918, after only four months' service, they were replaced by the Sopwith Dolphin. Fry's last victory with 23 Squadron, on 23 January 1918, was most likely *Leutnant* Walter von Bülow, commanding officer of *Jasta* Boelcke.

Leutnant Walter von Bülow

Born on 24 April 1894, von Bülow studied law at Heidelberg University. He served with Saxon Hussar Regiment Nr 17 and saw heavy fighting in the early part of the war. He then joined the flying service and was assigned to *FA*22, seeing action during late 1915 in the Champagne region. He spent most of 1916 with *FA*300 in Palestine, where he claimed three victories.

In early 1917 he was posted to *Jasta* 18 in the Ypres area, where he quickly claimed another nine Allied machines and received the Knight's Cross with Swords of the Hohenzollern House Order and the Saxon Military St Henry Order. His sixth victory, on 23 January 1917, was 41 Squadron's first casualty, Samuel Franklin Cody (*Ypres* page 176). In May he was promoted to leader of *Jasta* 36.

On 8 October 1917, with his claims having reached the total of 21, von Bülow was awarded the *Pour le Mérite*. The following month he was appointed to the command of the illustrious *Jasta* Boelcke. However, before he could add to his score of twenty-eight victories, he was shot down and killed by Willie Fry. Von Bülow's younger brother

Sixth from the left is Walter von Bülow, commander of *Jasta* 36. Eighth from the left is his brother Harry.

Harry, who also served in *Jasta* 36, as the surviving son, returned to the family estates in Holstein.

In his book Fry modestly wrote his account of the action:

> *On January 6th, 1918, our flight was on offensive patrol when we came across a tremendous battle between a large number of British and German scouts over the Passchendaele area, the British being mostly Camels. We joined in just as the fight was breaking up, with several machines in sight going down out of control and at least one in flames. My combat report states that we came across a formation of about five Albatros scouts flying west and that I dived on one, firing a burst of about twenty rounds from behind.*
>
> *The enemy aircraft at once rolled over and went down in a steep spiral and crashed in the shelled area south of Passchendaele. I was given credit for the machine as destroyed. Although the CO endorsed the combat report with the words 'confirmed by AA Group', I have always had a recollection that there was some question of a claim for the same machine made by pilots of the Camel Squadron. In general melées that sort of thing did arise.*
>
> *Just before the Second World War, Mr H. A. Jones, the RAF Official Historian, wrote to me asking if I could give any more*

information about the occurrence as it appears that the pilot of the German machine was Walter von Bülow, CO of the Jasta Boelcke at the time, which was news to me. I have since read that I have been given the credit for bringing down this distinguished pilot and CO, but have always been conscious that there was some question of other claims. In the circumstances, I would not wish to be given definite credit, especially as it was a confused fight.

William Mayes Fry

Willie Fry was born on 14 November 1896 and served in the ranks during the earliest days of the Great War. He participated in the famous Christmas truce of 1914. Posted back to the UK as he was underage, he returned to France in 1915, having been commissioned.

Joining the RFC at the end of 1915 he flew with 12 Squadron and then 11 Squadron. C Flight was absorbed into 60 Squadron, which he joined together with Albert Ball, later a famous ace and a Victoria Cross holder (*Arras* page 34). In this unit Fry was deputy leader to Billy Bishop, also later a VC holder and the highest scoring British and Commonwealth ace of the First World War (*Arras* page 142).

Having earned an MC, Fry was posted home at the end of June 1917. However he wanted to return to operations and in October he was sent to 23 Squadron. After an accident and

Willie Fry.

subsequent discharge from hospital, he was posted to 79 Squadron, who were equipped with the Sopwith Dolphin. He claimed his eleventh and last victory with this unit on 11 May 1918 but shortly after had another crash and was invalided home with 'Flying Sickness D' or flying exhaustion.

He had flown an amazing 637 hours, consisting of 381 operational sorties. He remained in the RAF between the wars before retiring in 1934 as a flight lieutenant. Serving throughout the Second World War, he finally retired on 15 July 1945 as a wing commander. He died on 4 August 1992.

After turning round, drive back to the road, and continue into Poperinge and return to Ypres. This completes the second tour.

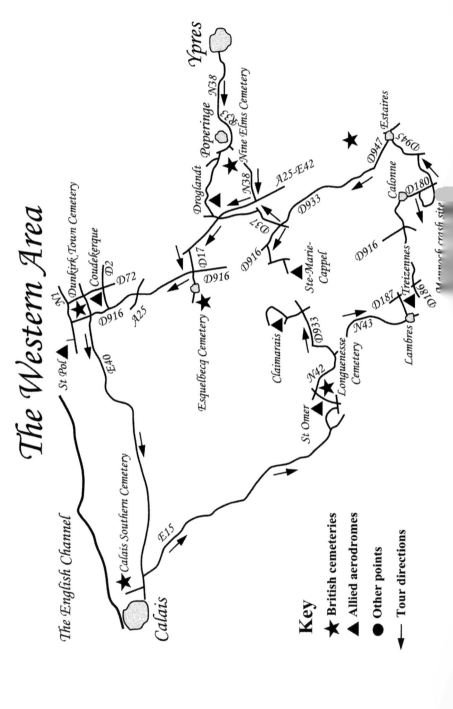

The Western Area

The English Channel

Ypres

Poperinge

Nine Elms Cemetery

Droglandt

N38

A25-E42

N38

D37

D933

D17

D916

Ste-Marie-Cappel

D947 Estaires

D945

Calonne

D180

D916

Mannock crash site

D187

Treizennes

D189

Lambres

N43

Longuenesse Cemetery

N42

St Omer

Claimarais

D933

Esquelbecq Cemetery

D916

A25

D916

D72

D2

Coudekerque

Dunkirk Town Cemetery

N1

St Pol

E40

E15

Calais Southern Cemetery

Calais

Key

★ British cemeteries
▲ Allied aerodromes
● Other points
→ Tour directions

Chapter Three

THE WESTERN AREA

Esquelbecq Cemetery	Herbert Musgrave
Coudekerque Aerodrome	Handley Page heavy bombers
Dunkirk Town Cemetery	G H Raleigh
St. Pol Aerodrome	Guynemer's last flight
Calais Southern Cemetery	H G Wanklyn
St Omer Aerodrome	The British Air Services Memorial
Longuenesse Souvenir Cemetery	John Cowell DCM, MM and Bar
Clairmarais Aerodrome	4 Australian Flying Corps
Treizennes Aerodrome	L W B Rees VC
Pacaut Wood	Mannock VC crash site
Ste-Marie-Cappel Aerodrome	45 Squadron
Droglandt Aerodrome	Raymond Collishaw Triplane ace
Nine Elms British Cemetery	The *Schlastas*

Leave Ypres on the N38 towards Poperinge. Around Poperinge on the ring road (R33), then left A25 Dunkirk. Join A25 Dunkirk/Calais. Leave motorway at Junction 15 Wormhout. Turn left, D17 Wormhout. In the village, cross the D916 on D17 Esquelbecq. Continue through Esquelbecq on the D17, and in the centre of the village pick up the green CWGC signs to the cemetery, which is beyond the village, down a lane to the left of the road.

Esquelbecq Military Cemetery

This cemetery (No. 26) was begun in April 1918 with the German spring offensive when the 2nd Canadian and 3rd Australian Casualty Clearing Stations moved here. It was closed in September 1918. Twenty-two years later it was utilised again during the retreat to Dunkirk in May 1940. The cemetery contains 578 burials from the First World War and 47 from the Second World War. There is a large open area in the far corner, which would have been Plot V but the US graves here were removed after the Armistice. Just beyond this space near the hedge is a single Indian grave and a row of eight German headstones.

Herbert Musgrave (III A1)

The grave we are visiting is in the farthest plot and is the first one in the front row, adjacent to the Stone of Remembrance.

Musgrave remains a largely unknown but, nonetheless, exceedingly influential figure in the progress of the RFC and ultimately the RAF. With his inquisitive mind and inventiveness, he was instrumental in the development of wireless, an essential ingredient of artillery ranging. His contribution to the expansion of military flying in Great Britain has been sadly underestimated.

Born on 11 May 1876 in Adelaide, South Australia, he was the younger son of Sir Anthony Musgrave, Governor of New South Wales. Educated at Harrow he entered the army and was commissioned a second lieutenant in the Royal Engineers on 1 March 1898. He served throughout the South African or Boer War and was twice Mentioned in Despatches, receiving the Queen's Medal with five clasps and the King's Medal with two clasps. After three years with the South African Constabulary, he returned to the UK and attended Staff College, following which he was posted to Malta on staff duties. He had

Major Herbert Musgrave.

an inquiring mind and was a regular contributor to a number of military publications on a wide variety of subjects.

As a result of the crossing of the English Channel by Louis Blériot in 1909, Musgrave's mind was fired by the military possibilities and he drew the War Office's attention to it. Such was his enthusiasm for aviation he learned to fly during a period of leave and gained his Royal Aero Club certificate, No. 357, flying a Bristol Biplane, on 12 November 1912. He had already tried to join the RFC but it was not until December 1912 that he was posted to them at Farnborough. In March 1913 he was gazetted a squadron commander.

Promoted to the post of Assistant Commandant and Officer in Charge of Experiments, he was involved with every technical aspect of the RFC, from kite balloons through to photography, wireless, bomb dropping and co-operation with artillery. In April 1914 a headquarters flight was put under his command. Apart from being concerned with technical matters he was also closely involved with the administration of the RFC, including its plans for mobilisation. He was responsible for much of the planning and administration of the RFC's Concentration Camp in July 1914, during which there was a programme of training, lectures and practical tests involving many of the skills which would be required in the event of war.

On the outbreak of hostilities, much to his dismay, Musgrave was seconded to the War Office as deputy to the Assistant Director of Military Aeronautics, Sefton Brancker. However his tenure was short, as his services were required by HQ RFC in France. Here he spent his time overseeing a variety of equipment and allied technical matters, including wireless telegraphy. He encouraged the work of B T James and D S Lewis on the 'clock-code' method of ranging artillery (*Ypres* page 39).

His greatest contribution was in the field of wireless telegraphy. On 27 September 1914, the Headquarters Wireless Telegraphy Unit (HQ WTU) was formed under his command to meet the rapidly growing needs for wireless-equipped aeroplanes. Two months later its title was changed to No. 9 (Wireless) Squadron and Musgrave was the first commander, with James and Lewis as his flight commanders. It was from this beginning that the entire RFC/RAF wireless telegraphy organisation developed for the rest of war.

Unfortunately it is from this same period that there are two written accounts of Musgrave that are less than flattering. Two of Musgrave's junior officers were J T C Moore-Brabazon, holder of Royal Aero Club certificate No.1 (later Lord Brabazon of Tara) and H C T Dowding (later Air Chief Marshal Lord Dowding). Undoubtedly there was a clash of personalities between three exceedingly strong characters. But there is no doubt that Musgrave was held in high regard by his seniors as was shown by the letters of condolence following his death.

Like a number of officers seconded to the RFC from their parent regiments or corps, Musgrave felt he should return to the Royal Engineers. On 17 February 1915 he was Mentioned in Despatches again and received the DSO. The following month he returned to staff duties, being appointed a Deputy Quarter Master General. In May 1916 he was on the staff of the 24th Division in order to gain front line experience but was severely wounded in the August. On 27 December 1917 he returned to the Western Front as an intelligence staff officer with HQ II Corps in the Ypres area. While attached to 2/Irish Rifles for three days, he accompanied a night patrol on 2 June 1918. Lying in a shell hole he was mortally wounded by a rifle grenade. His body was brought back, but why to a cemetery so far behind the lines is a mystery.

War in the Air, the official history of the Royal Air Force in the First World War, contains what would, perhaps, have been a suitable epitaph:

> *He desired no personal advancement, and would have thought no other honour so great as to die for his country. Such men, though the records of their lives are buried under a mass of tedious detail, are the engineers of victory.*

For those readers who would like to know more about Musgrave and the activities of No. 9 (Wireless Squadron), I would suggest three excellent articles in the journal of *Cross and Cockade International* by Peter Dye, volume 27 page 203 and volume 35 pages 95 and 106.

Return to Wormhout, and turn left on D916 Quaëdypre. Follow D916, through Quaëdypre, over the motorway and through Bergues. Continue northwards on D916, then turn right over the canal bridge D2 Coudekerque Village, then left on D72 Coudekerque Branche. Look for the farm on the left side of the road, with a bridge over the canal just beyond the farm buildings. Drive over the bridge and park.

Coudekerque Aerodrome

This site is important in that a number of RNAS units were formed here – 4 Naval, 5 Naval, 14 Naval and 15 Naval Squadrons. The only non-naval unit to be stationed here was 98 Squadron with their DH9s, in May 1918.

On 31 December 1916 No. 4 Naval was formed from 'A' Squadron of No. 5 Naval Wing, initially equipped with Sopwith 1½ Strutters and Sopwith Pups but ultimately with the Sopwith Camel. On the same day 5 Naval was established from 'B' Squadron, also of 5 Naval Wing.

Picture No.19. Coudekerque in 2002 looking north.

Coudekerque Aerodrome

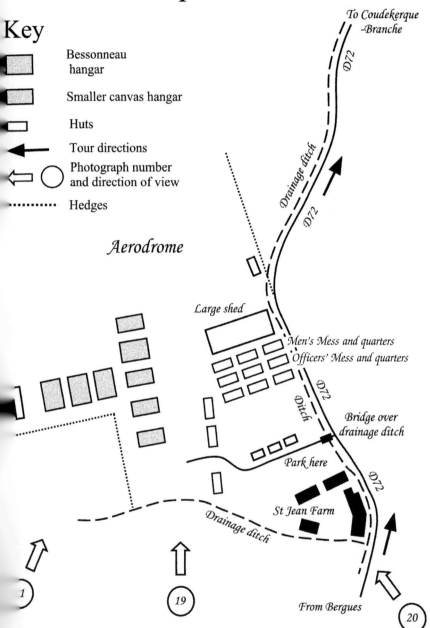

Key

Bessonneau hangar

Smaller canvas hangar

Huts

Tour directions

Photograph number and direction of view

Hedges

To Coudekerque -Branche

D72

D72

Drainage ditch

Aerodrome

Large shed

Men's Mess and quarters

Officers' Mess and quarters

D72

Ditch

Bridge over drainage ditch

Park here

D72

St Jean Farm

Drainage ditch

1

19

From Bergues

20

Picture No.20. Looking northwest during the First World War. Visible are a number of Handley Pages.

They commenced operations with Sopwith 1½ Strutters but re-equipped with De Havilland DH4, then DH9as.

However Coudekerque is better associated with the other two naval units formed here. On 31 December 1916 No.7 Naval Squadron was constituted at Petite-Synthe from 'B' Squadron of 4 Naval Wing. In July 1917 the unit was split into two, forming 7 and 7A (Naval) Squadrons. On 9 December 1917 No. 14 Naval Squadron was formed from 7A, employing Handley Page 0/100s. They were to remain at Coudekerque, apart from a short break in March 1918, until June of the same year.

No. 15 Naval Squadron formed here on 10 March 1918 from a nucleus of 7 Naval and 14 Naval, also flying the HP 0/100. They stayed at Coudekerque until April, when they were sent to the UK, re-

Picture No. 21. An unusual shot of a Handley Page of 7 Squadron landing at Coudekerque on 7 June 1917, with the King of Belgium aboard.

Handley Page 3116, 'B3' of 7 Naval. This was the first 0/100 delivered to the unit on 4 March 1917.

equipping with the HP 0/400 before becoming part of the Independent Force, based near Verdun attacking targets in Germany.

The introduction of the Handley-Page 0/100, the first true heavy bomber the British flying services received, is described in *Airfields and Airmen; Ypres*, page 177.

The two Handley Page units at Coudekerque attacked as many targets as possible, weather and engine problems permitting. Some nights up to eight of these giant machines were sent out. Primary targets were docks, railways and gun batteries. On 29/30 May 1918, No. 214 Squadron (as 14 Naval had become) despatched six HPs to bomb Bruges docks. The next night they sent eight machines on a repeat attack on the docks and the nearby Le Brugeois Works. Nearly eleven tons of bombs were dropped in the two raids. Information was later received that a munitions depot had had several sections destroyed, killing about 200 soldiers. In addition two large torpedo boats were blown up in Bruges docks.

Losses to enemy action were light, the main enemy being the weather, making night flying hazardous. Other problems were poor aerodromes, which were too small and frequently rain-sodden. In addition landing aids were virtually non-existent for machines returning in bad weather. Two machines were shot down during May. On the night of 15/16 May 1918 HP 3132 was brought down by anti-aircraft fire and the crew killed (*Ypres* page 178). Three nights later C3487 failed to return and the crew were also killed (page 53).

In June 1918 214 Squadron left Coudekerque and, as the enemy retreated in late 1918, they moved forward twice more. Their last operation was on the night of 10/11 November 1918, when they despatched seven HPs against Louvain railway station.

After the last operational unit, 98 Squadron, left in early June 1918 Coudekerque became No. 11 Aircraft Park, servicing the squadrons of No. 5 (Operations) Group.

145

The tailfin of a
1650 lb SN bomb,
giving some idea
of its size.

The other ranks' mess at Coudekerque.

The explosive casing of a
1650 lb SN bomb.

Continue north on the D72, over the motorway. Proceed ahead, over the railway, keeping the canal on your left. The cemetery comes into view on your right, continue northwards until turning right into the entrance to the main civilian cemetery at the green CWGC sign and park. You will see green CWGC signs to the left, pointing to the Dunkirk Memorial, which is a five minute walk down the main road.

Dunkirk Town Cemetery

The British Expeditionary Force landed at Dunkirk in September and October 1914 and the area remained an important base throughout the war, despite being constantly bombed and shelled. It was also a French hospital centre. There are 460 burials from the Great War and 793 as a result of the Second World War. The town was the scene of the historic evacuation of the BEF in May 1940.

As you enter the main entrance to the Memorial, on the right are Plots I and II from the Second World War, with Plots IV and V, consisting of First World War burials beyond. In the public cemetery adjacent to the CWGC site are First World War Plots I, II and III.

The centre piece of the cemetery (No.19) is the Dunkirk Memorial, which you walk through as you enter. It was designed by Philip Hepworth and the engraved panel shows the evacuation by John Hutton. The memorial panels on either side of the path commemorate the 4,500 casualties of the 1939 – 1940 campaign who have no known grave. The first casualty we are interested in is commemorated on the bottom of the first panel on the right (panel two).

Major George Douglas Hill

Though a First World War pilot, Hill is commemorated as a Second World War casualty who has no known grave.

Born on 22 September 1891 at Southampton, Hill was commissioned into the 7th Hussars on 9 September 1911, promotion to lieutenant following on 10 March 1913. He joined the RFC and was posted to No. 7 Squadron which was reforming on 28 September 1914. They had been disbanded on 8 August in order to supply personnel for the squadrons proceeding to France. He went overseas with them to

Major G D Hill, commanding 27 Squadron.

147

DH9 D506 'H'of 27 Squadron. This machine served with the unit from August 1918 until passed on to 98 Squadron in March 1919.

St Omer on 8 April 1915 as an observer. After learning to fly at the Le Crotoy school on the estuary of the River Somme he obtained his Royal Aero Club 'ticket', No. 1783, on 22 September 1915, flying a Maurice Farman. Returning in October to the UK, he was sent to 18 Squadron for further instruction as a pilot.

On 20 August 1916 Hill was posted to 40 Squadron as a flight commander, initially at St. Omer, then Treizennes (page 175). Unfortunately his stay was brief as he was injured in an accident on 1 November whilst flying an FE8. Returning to England, he spent 1917 instructing with 82 Squadron and the Central Flying School.

In August 1917 he was promoted to squadron commander and on 13 March 1918 crossed to France to take command of 27 Squadron. They were operating the Airco DH4 and were based at Villers-Bretonneux (*Somme* page 130). It was not a good time for Hill to assume command as the great German spring offensive started only a week after his arrival and within days they had to retreat in the face of the rapid enemy advance. By the time of the Armistice the squadron had moved aerodromes seven times. On 20 March 1919 Hill returned to the UK and was placed on the RAF unemployed list before returning to his regiment on 26 May 1919. For his services he was Mentioned in Despatches on 11 July 1919.

On 8 July 1930 he was transferred to the regular reserve of officers with the rank of major.

He was killed on Monday 20 May 1940. Unfortunately it has proved impossible to find which unit he was attached to in France – his parent regiment, the 7th Hussars, were serving in Egypt at the time.

Henry Ridewood Foden (IV C5)

The next grave we are visiting is situated in the far right corner, third row from the back and is the seventh grave from the far end. Swinging a propeller in order to start an engine is a dangerous past-time. Considering how many times this procedure was carried out during the war and the number of machines manoeuvring on aerodromes, it is amazing how few accidents there were. Foden was probably the only person killed or died of injuries whilst swinging a propeller in the British flying services during the First World War.

Born on 5 March 1894 in Bristol, Foden had been a fitter in civilian life. Joining the navy on 15 May 1915, he was promoted to air mechanic first class from 2 July 1918. He had been a member of the Seaplane Defence Flight before it became 13 Naval then 213 Squadron.

On 18 July 1918 he was turning the engine of Sopwith Camel D8147 of 213 Squadron at Bergues. Even though the magnetos were switched off, the engine fired after six or seven turns. The result was that Foden's right forearm was severed and later amputated further up the arm due to elbow damage. In addition he had lacerations of the left hand and head, plus contused and abrased injuries to the left thigh, left knee and face. He was taken by car to the 202 Squadron sick bay and then to Queen Alexandria Hospital, Petite-Synthe, in a dangerous condition. He died the following day. Air Mechanic Second Class B G Watts, who was also helping, had the presence of mind to push against the boss of the propeller and was flung three or four yards away.

It was found that the contact between the earth wire connection and the central screw of the contact breaker was 'indifferent' in the starboard magneto. This was changed and tested OK. No blame was attached to Sergeant J H Pearson who was sat in the pilot's seat at the time of the accident.

George Hebden Raleigh (I A1)

The second grave we are visiting is next door, in Plot I of the civilian section. Return to the civilian cemetery. The British plots are to your right, from the main entrance. The burial is in the front row on the left hand end.

Raleigh has the dubious distinction of being the first in a long list of British squadron commanders to be killed in the First World War. He was born on 30 June 1878 in Melbourne and was commissioned as a second lieutenant in the Essex Regiment on 15 November 1899. Promotion to captain occurred on 8 January 1908. He learned to fly at Brooklands and was awarded his Royal Aero Club certificate, No. 196, on 12 March 1912, flying a Bristol biplane. The following month he joined the Air Battalion of the Royal Engineers,

G H Raleigh, the first RFC squadron commander to be killed.

which became the Royal Flying Corps on 13 May 1912. Promoted to brevet major on 22 June 1914 he was commanding No. 4 Squadron at the outbreak of war. On 13 August 1914 he was one of that happy band of RFC pioneers who crossed to France.

P B Joubert de la Ferté (later Air Chief Marshal Sir Philip, KCB, CMG, DSO), a flight commander in 3 Squadron, wrote in his diary on 27 September 1914:

> *Comic yarn about Raleigh. He was out late last night, & landed out in the country, taking a sunken road & telegraph wires in his stride, so to speak. No damage to the machine. He came back early this morning, as he loomed up through the fog, one of No. 4's mechanics was heard to say 'No bloody luck, here he is back again'.*

On 21 January 1915 Raleigh was killed when flying a Vickers FB5 off the Belgian coast.

From the cemetery entrance, turn left along the main road (N1), and pick up signs for St. Pol-sur-Mer. Follow the signs through the traffic complex in the centre of Dunkerque until passing under a railway bridge. Bear right at the next junction for St. Pol-sur-Mer, and at the next traffic lights turn right for Maison de Quartier de l'Ile Jeanty. Continue to the T-junction and turn right. Over the first iron bridge turn immediate left, and continue as far as possible, keeping the water on your left. Park at the end.

St. Pol Aerodrome

This historic site has now largely disappeared under industrial re-development. It was both a British and French aerodrome and is of particular interest to us as being the one from which the great French ace Georges Guynemer took off on his last and fatal flight. His career was described in *Ypres* page 142.

Guynemer was serving in *Spa*3, which was part of *Groupe de Combat* 12 (*GC*12) or *les Cignones* (Storks), as they were known after their unit emblem. The *Spa* designator indicated that they were operating Spad aircraft, having previously been *N*3 when they had flown Nieuport machines. The *groupe* had been on the French sector but, together with *GC*11 and *GC*13, they were moved north on 11 July 1917 to bolster the permanent *escadrille*, *N*102, on the French 1*ère Armée* front. Initially based at Bierne, west of Berques, *Spa* 3, *Spa* 26, *Spa* 73 and *Spa* 103 then moved to St. Pol-sur-Mer on 12 August 1917. The increase in French air power was to assist the British offensive in

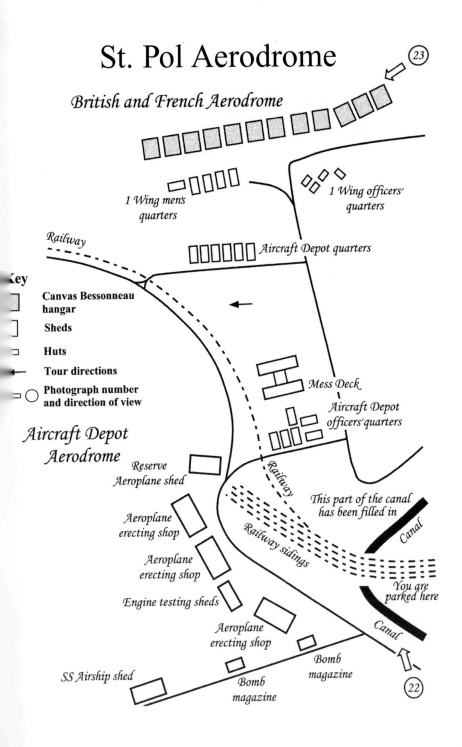

St. Pol Aerodrome

23

British and French Aerodrome

1 Wing men's quarters

1 Wing officers' quarters

Railway

Aircraft Depot quarters

Key

Canvas Bessonneau hangar

Sheds

Huts

Tour directions

Photograph number and direction of view

Aircraft Depot Aerodrome

Mess Deck

Aircraft Depot officers' quarters

Reserve Aeroplane shed

Railway

Aeroplane erecting shop

This part of the canal has been filled in

Canal

Railway sidings

Aeroplane erecting shop

You are parked here

Engine testing sheds

Aeroplane erecting shop

Canal

SS Airship shed

Bomb magazine

Bomb magazine

22

Picture No.22. St. Pol looking northwest in 2005.

Flanders, known later as Passchendaele, which began on 31 July 1917.

At the end of July Guynemer took temporary command of *N3* when the commanding officer, *Capitaine* Alfred Auger, was killed (Somme page 131). He again assumed command of the unit when *Capitaine* Albert Hertaux was severely wounded.

During this period on the northern front Guynemer would claim his last five victories, numbers 49 to 53, of which four were gained using a Spad fitted with a fearsome 37 mm single-shot cannon.

Picture No. 23. St. Pol looking southwest during the First World War. The hangars of the British/French aerodrome can be seen extending away to the right.

On the morning of 11 September 1917 Guynemer, *Sous-Lieutenant* Jean Bozon-Verduraz and *Sergent* Louis Risacher prepared for a patrol. Unfortunately, despite the best efforts of his mechanics, the engine on Risacher's machine would not start, so at 0835 hours Guynemer and Bozon-Verduraz departed St. Pol on their own. It was a misty morning but at 5,000 feet the pair broke out into bright sunshine. An hour after getting airborne they spotted a Rumpler reconnaissance machine at 12,000 feet near Poelkappelle. Guynemer dived on it but missed and Bozon-Verduraz following behind also failed to hit it as the German machine had gone in to a spin heading for the mist below. Guynemer pursued the enemy machine but, while checking the surrounding area, Bozon-Verduraz sighted what he thought were eight German scouts approaching and turned towards them. They either failed to notice the Spads or chose not to attack, as the

Georges Guynemer in front of a Spad.

formation then turned away east. Bozon-Verduraz returned to where he had last seen Guynemer but there was no sign of him. He continued his patrol alone and landed back at St. Pol at 1020 hours to find Guynemer had not returned.

One of the units opposing the Allies was *Jasta* 3, based at Rumbeke, on the southern outskirts of Roulers. Among its successful pilots was Georg Schlenker, whose first victory had been the commanding officer of 52 Squadron RFC, Major Leonard Parker (*Cambrai*, page 141). Another up and coming fighter pilot was Kurt Wissemann. At 0910 hours on the morning of 11 September four Albatros DVs took off from Rumbeke. Wissemann described the action:

> *At 0950 I was attacked by a French single-seater east of St. Julien. I was able to frustrate the attack by turning away. My opponent refused combat, but instead dived past me heading towards the Front. In the next instant, I moved in directly behind the enemy machine and opened fire. As a result of my shooting, the aircraft turned over sideways several times, then began spinning down in very tight*

153

***Leutnant* Kurt Wissemann, *Jasta* 3, probable victor over Georges Guynemer.**

circles. The dive increased with such speed that it was impossible for me to follow, but I continued watching the spinning machine to about 1500 metres where it became lost in the haze. As to the aircraft, what particularly struck me was its brilliant markings. I distinctly recognized the French national insignia, an observation which several men of my Staffel also reported soon after landing. The crash site lies in range of enemy fire about two kilometres north of Gravenstafel. There likewise on the morning of 12 September Unteroffizier Kahmann discovered a shot-down French Spad.

It is to be assumed with reasonable certainty that the occupant of the enemy aircraft is identical with that of the French Capitaine Guynemer. Further inquiries are being conducted by the Flieger-Verfolgungsstafel.

Four days later in a letter to his parents he wrote:

On September 11, by the way, I downed my fifth opponent. It was really clever. I flew alone towards the Front acting as if I were a completely harmless passerby. My opponent fell for the ruse, left his Geschwader and attacked me from above. At first, I calmly let him approach, then as he came near enough to be in range, I made a sharp bank so that he flew by me unable to shoot. In the next moment I sat close behind him and with comparatively few shots brought him down. He lies between the positions near St. Julien, south of Langemarck.

Medical orderlies from *Infanterie Regiment* 413 reached the wreckage, which was badly smashed, and found the pilot's body nearby. Apart from other injuries he appeared to have been shot through the head. They found several items, one of which was Guynemer's identity card. Unfortunately, the Germans troops were about to be replaced by another unit and so his remains were left where they fell. Whether the new regiment buried him is not known but within a very short time Allied artillery fire would have obliterated any sign of pilot and machine.

Kurt Wissemann

Born on 20 March 1893 in Elberfeld, Wissemann joined up in August 1914. Serving with the Marburg *Reserve-Jäger-Bataillon* Nr. 11, he was on active service during the German army's sweep through France and was awarded the Iron Cross Second Class. Commissioned in March 1915, he participated in the fighting around Verdun in early 1916. Tiring of life in the trenches, Wissemann applied to the air service and, after training, joined *Flieger Abteilung* 31 in September.

154

Wissemann's Albatros DV after a slight mishap in September 1917.

Bored with two-seater reconnaissance work he applied for fighter pilot training and after a period at *Jastaschule Valenciennes* (*Cambrai* page 33) was posted to *Jasta* 3 on 28 May 1917.

A little over a month after Wissemann's arrival he claimed his first Allied machine when he shot down a Bristol Fighter of 48 Squadron, whose crew were both killed. In August he claimed a Camel, a Nieuport and a Spad. His fifth and last claim was Georges Guynemer. On 28 September Wissemann's luck ran out when he was shot down and killed over Westroobeke. As with many claims, it is difficult to be completely sure who shot him down, but it would seem he fell to pilots

Three pilots from 56 Squadron. Left to right, R T C Hoidge, G H Bowman and R A Maybery. Wissemann possibly fell victim to either Hoidge or Bowman.

of 56 Squadron RFC. His body was returned to Germany and buried in his home town, near Dusseldorf.

In recent times there has been doubt concerning Wissemann's claim, some of it generated by the various times quoted, with the added confusion that during certain periods German and Allied times were different. There is a theory that while attacking the two-seater Guynemer was wounded and then finished off by Wissemann.

Marco Fernandez-Sommerau in Belgium has the remains of Rumpler CIV 1463/17, which was shot down later in the day by Maurice Medaerts of the Belgian *5me Escadrille*. Marco believes that this may have been the machine involved in the Guynemer incident. Because it was destroyed and the crew killed they were obviously unable to put in a claim for the great French ace.

Return to the NI. Cross the NI, then continue left towards the church with two spires. After passing under the railway bridge, but before reaching the church, turn right on the D916 Coudekerque Branche. Stay on the D916 to the motorway, and turn right E40 Calais. Continue on E40 and leave for Calais Car Ferry. At the next junction, Junction 3 Calais Centre, leave the motorway and from the roundabout follow Calais Centre. Turn left at the first roundabout, and right at the next. The cemetery will come into view on the left, behind a high wall. From the main entrance, follow the small CWGC signs to the British military plot, which is in the far left corner of the civilian cemetery.

Calais Southern Cemetery

During the Great War Calais was an important centre for the British forces. In April 1915 No. 6 Base Depot was established here to ease the pressure on Boulogne and also to provide a supply centre that was nearer the Front than Rouen or Le Havre. It remained operating until the last British forces finally left France in March 1921. In addition the 30th, 35th and 38th General Hospitals, No. 9 British Red Cross Hospital and No. 10 Canadian Stationary Hospital were based in the town. This cemetery (No. 7) was in use from May 1915 to March 1918. Subsequently, further burials were made at the new Les Baraques Cemetery (No. 6). There are 721 First World War graves, plus 224 from the Second World War as a result of the fighting during the evacuation of France in May 1940.

H G Wanklyn

There are only two Great War fliers graves here and the one we are visiting is against the boundary hedge at the end of the row on the right hand side. It is easily distinguished as it has a non-standard headstone. This is Plot A, Officers' Row, Grave 1. Unusually the plots have letters rather than Roman numerals as in most other Commonwealth War Graves Commission cemeteries.

This casualty is of particular interest as he is an early RNAS fatality and he has a non-standard headstone. These are rare, especially for airmen.

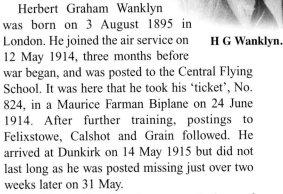

H G Wanklyn.

Herbert Graham Wanklyn was born on 3 August 1895 in London. He joined the air service on 12 May 1914, three months before war began, and was posted to the Central Flying School. It was here that he took his 'ticket', No. 824, in a Maurice Farman Biplane on 24 June 1914. After further training, postings to Felixstowe, Calshot and Grain followed. He arrived at Dunkirk on 14 May 1915 but did not last long as he was posted missing just over two weeks later on 31 May.

Wanklyn's non-standard headstone. The inscription is on the base.

Wanklyn took off at the very early hour of 0330 for a patrol to Ostend in Maurice Farman Pusher Seaplane No.114. Whether he was shot down by ground defences or suffered an engine failure is unknown but his body was found in the sea nearly three weeks later on 17 June.

Maurice Farman Seaplane No. 114 in which Wanklyn went missing.

Return to the motorway, and go south on the E15 St. Omer. Leave at Junction 3 St. Omer, and at the roundabout continue ahead for Wizernes. Turn left onto the D211 Wizernes. In Wizernes, turn left at the T-junction, D928 St. Omer Longuenesse, and left again at the next T-junction. Continue ahead, up the hill, and the airfield will come into view on your left. At the far end of the airfield, turn left on the D198 Longuenesse to the aerodrome. Take the first left turn to the monument.

St. Omer Aerodrome

From the RFC point of view this spot was its spiritual home. From small beginnings in 1914, by 1918 it had become a huge, sprawling establishment and had taken over the entire town of St. Omer. It was a vast aircraft depot, bustling with energy. New aeroplanes were delivered here, broken machines re-built, captured German aeroplanes analysed and new squadrons arrived here first. In addition it had the Pilots' Pool, where new pilots awaited their postings to squadrons. Just about every man and woman of the RFC/RAF passed through at some time, with many visiting it several times.

On 26 July 1918 the legendary Major Mick Mannock, later awarded the VC, took off from here on his last fatal flight (*Arras* page 34). Billy Bishop VC, who commanded 85 Squadron before Mannock, claimed the last twelve of his total of seventy-two victories while based here. In addition, J A Liddell took off from the aerodrome to earn the fourth Victoria Cross awarded to an airman.

Picture No.24. St. Omer in 2005 looking due east.

St. Omer

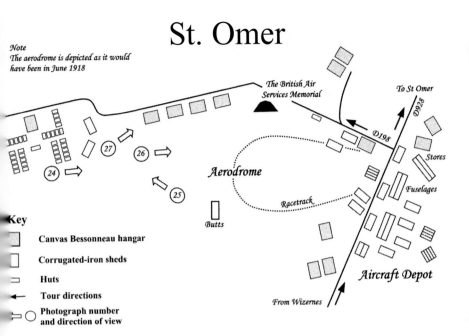

The British Air Services Memorial

To St Omer

D228

D198

Stores

Aerodrome

27

26

24

25

Racetrack

Fuselages

Butts

Key

Canvas Bessonneau hangar

Corrugated-iron sheds

Huts

Tour directions

Photograph number and direction of view

Aircraft Depot

From Wizernes

Picture No.25. St. Omer during the First World War looking northwest, with the RE8s of 4 Squadron.

The British Air Services Memorial, unveiled on 11 September 2004.

The British Air Services Memorial

In *Airfields and Airmen; Arras* I wrote about the proposed memorial to the British Air Services, which was to be unveiled at St. Omer. I also voiced my opinion about the Air Force's Memorial to the Missing at Arras.

Though there has been a memorial to the missing of the RAF and its predecessors since July 1932, there has been no such commemoration to the others who were killed and have a grave, or to the many thousands of men and women who served their country in the air services during the Great War.

Under the auspices of *Cross and Cockade International* and its president, Air Vice-Marshal Peter Dye, this has now been corrected and the new memorial was dedicated on 11 September 2004. The ceremony was well attended with all the dignitaries from the town of St. Omer and senior officers of the Royal Air Force and *l'Armée de l'Air*, plus a flypast by both services. At long last the British and Empire air service personnel have a fitting tribute; and on the most relevant and important site.

Maurice Baring wrote in his book *Flying Corps H.Q. 1914-1918* of the early days of the headquarters at St. Omer:

> *We arrived at St. Omer at 8.30, and took up our residence in a small château on the hill between the town and the aerodrome. We didn't expect to stay there long, so no real steps were taken to make ourselves comfortable at the start. The château was a modern stucco building, red and white. Downstairs there were two drawing-rooms, a dining-room, and one bedroom, and a small sitting-room. The small sitting-room was Colonel Sykes' office. One of the drawing-rooms was made into an ante-room, the other into the office. The bedroom downstairs was Brooke-Popham's. Upstairs General Henderson had one big bedroom and a small office. Salmond, B.K. and I shared a second, Murat had a third, and the fourth was to be occupied by other members of staff.*
>
> *We sadly overcrowded this house. In the office B.K. used to*

sit at one table (a card table), Salmond at another rickety piece of furniture. Brooke-Popham had a second small card table for his work, which soon became littered with papers. The Sergeant-Major sat on a box in front of other boxes. A bevy of clerks filled the room. Each clerk had a typewriter, and each clerk's box had about a dozen candles stuck on to it burning and guttering. The atmosphere was quite solid. We thought on arriving that we were going to stop here a few days. As it turned out this little château was the R.F.C. headquarters until 1916 and again in 1917, and until the end of the war it was always occupied by an R.F.C. staff.

Picture No.26. The SE5as of 85 Squadron shortly before Mannock took command. In the far distance can be seen the various workshops, stores and offices of the aircraft depot. The nearest SE5a, C1904 'Z', was flown by Billy Bishop VC and he claimed his last twelve victories with it.

Sykes was General Staff Officer Grade 1 and later Major-General Sir Frederick. Brooke-Popham was Deputy Assistant Quartermaster General and later Air Chief Marshal Sir Robert (*Cambrai* page 50). General Sir David Henderson was commanding the RFC. Salmond was a GSO 2 and later Air Chief Marshal Sir Geoffrey. Murat was the French liaison officer. B K was B H Barrington-Kennett, the RFC adjutant who was later killed in action, (*Arras* page 86).

Baring again:

At St. Omer quite a new kind of life began for us. The war began to settle, although we were unaware of the fact, for when we got there the race to the sea was not over, and the battle of the Yser had not yet been fought. But everything became more

161

Picture No.27. Captain D F Stevenson DSO MC (left) and his observer, Lieutenant J W Baker MC with their RE8 of 4 Squadron. Stevenson retired as an air vice-marshal and Baker as an air chief marshal.

regular; books used to arrive. And a great quantity of guests used to stream through the house. In fact, someone said our château was exactly like a Dak bungalow, whatever that may be. It was certainly like a damp bungalow. Pilots, observers, staff-officers, administrative officers, experts, etc., used to arrive from London, and sometimes from Paris, and sometimes from the sky, and stay the night. They used to sleep on the floor of our bedrooms in their valises. Sometimes there were as many as five officers in one bedroom. It was no place for those who like privacy. Personally I enjoyed this perpetual ebb and flow of guests.

My main recollection of that first period of St. Omer is a stuffy office, full of clerks and candles and a deafening noise of typewriters. A constant stream of pilots arriving in the evening in burberries with maps talking over reconnaissances; a perpetual stream of guests and a crowd of people sleeping on the floor; a weekly struggle, sometimes successful and sometimes not, to get a bath in the town, where there was always a seething crowd of suppliants, and a charming, capable lady in charge who used to call one 'Mon très cher Monsieur'; hours spent on the Aerodrome, which were generally misty; and small dinners in the Flight messes in the various billets round Longuenesse, and almost every day some inquiry or dispute with regard to a billet.

R R Money wrote of the early days of the aerodrome and personalities in his autobiography *Flying and Soldiering*:

The presence of the School at St. Omer led to our meeting many pilots from other Squadrons and from home. The School had a Martinsyde Scout, a B.E.2.A., and one or two other old veterans; and budding Bristol Scout pilots came to practise on

162

the Martinsyde, while such pilots as were short of practice, or not too clever, made use of the other machines. In addition, St. Omer held in those days the only Aircraft Depot in France, where new machines from England were collected and tested before going on to the Squadrons. So we met the ferry pilots, and those from the Squadrons who came to collect their machines.

Moore-Brabazon, who was then at the head of the Photographic Section, was another who made St. Omer his headquarters at that time. So did the Honourable Maurice Baring, who had a post under Trenchard at R.F.C. H.Q. He ran the Mess there, excellently well, of course, and we accused him of having nothing else to do. He cost us most of our liqueur glasses one night, since he would insist on adding just one more to a toppling pile of them which he had built on the dining-table. Only the other day I saw a reference in a weekly paper to his skill in balancing something or other on his bald head. So the years fly by. He was not bald in 1915.

A Squadron of the Royal Flying Corps was entitled to the use of riding horses, and G.H.Q. stables were instructed to send horses up for our use when required. As the aerodrome was formerly the steeplechase course, and most of the jumps were still in situ, we made full use of our opportunities. My usual mount, a black, had, the groom assured me, been a Grand National horse. I don't believe it now, and I don't know how he should know anyway, but I was pleased to believe it at the time. He was a fine jumper, but, I think, too small for the Aintree Course. Unfortunately, one or two horses were badly handled, or the grooms were insufficiently fee'd, and G.H.Q. refused to send us their own horses any longer, and turned us on to the North Irish Horse. I do not know whether these gentlemen took our measure, or whether they really were the world's worst mounted Cavalry Regiment, but...!!

Be2b of 4 Squadron at St. Omer.

John Aidan Liddell VC

As mentioned earlier, among the many incidents that involved airmen based here was the action for which J A Liddell earned the fourth Victoria Cross awarded to an airman.

The eldest of three sons, Liddell was born on 3 August 1888. He suffered from delicate health, which handicapped his activities. In September 1900 he entered Stonyhouse College, where he distinguished himself in science classes. He had a natural bent for anything mechanical, though he was also a keen observer and lover of nature. His interests were varied, and included chemistry, music, photography and astronomy. At Balliol College, Oxford, where he was known as Peter, he secured an honours degree in zoology. After leaving Oxford he joined the special reserve of officers 3rd Battalion Argyll and Sutherland Highlanders in 1911. His interest in mechanical things led him to take up flying and on 14 May 1914 he passed his 'ticket', No. 781, with the Vickers Flying School at Brooklands. At the outbreak of war, having been promoted to captain, Liddell went to France with the 2nd Battalion, and his responsibility was the machine gun sections. He was in constant action throughout the winter until he went back to England for leave on 11 January 1915. When he returned to his battalion he was feeling rather seedy, with a sore throat and pains in his back, legs and head.

On 28 January Liddell was invalided home and at a medical board on 3 March it was noted he had recovered from influenza but was suffering from rheumatism in the right shoulder from standing in wet trenches. For his devotion to duty and courage he was awarded the MC in January 1915 and Mentioned in Despatches.

Seconded to the RFC, Liddell arrived at Shoreham on 3 May 1915 for flying tuition. Following more training at Dover, he was posted to 7 Squadron in France on 24 July 1915, joining A Flight. He flew his first patrol on 29 July, reconnoitring the area around Ostend and Bruges, during which he had a number of inconclusive scraps with enemy machines.

His second operational flight proved to be his last. On 31 July he departed flying an RE5 for another reconnaissance in the Ostend – Bruges area. In the RE5 the observer occupied the front cockpit.

J A Liddell VC.

Liddell's observer, Second Lieutenant R H Peck, was armed with a Lewis machine gun and a service rifle. While over Bruges they were fired on from above by a German tractor biplane. Peck fired a full drum of ammunition but was then nearly thrown out of the machine as it fell on its back. Hanging on to a strut he was unable to do anything until the machine suddenly righted itself. In the rear cockpit Liddell had been badly wounded by the German's last burst of fire. His right thigh was ripped open to the bone, where it had been gouged away. Also the machine was difficult to fly because of the damage. Liddell could easily have landed to have his terrible wound attended to, but he indicated to Peck that he intended to land on the beach, west of Nieuport. Peck suggested the Belgian aerodrome at Furnes as being a better option (page 124).

Flying for over half an hour and unable to use the throttle he landed at full power, switching off just before touching down. While waiting for a doctor to arrive Liddell applied a splint and tourniquet to his own leg. He was taken to the hospital at La Panne, where he remained for the next month.

Lieutenant Dhanis of the *Aviation Militaire Belge* wrote to Major Hoare, commanding 7 Squadron on 1 August 1915:

> *I, the undersigned, Dhanis, of the 1st Regiment of the Guides, Flight Lieut. and Commandant of the 3rd Escadrille of the Belgian Flying Corps, consider it my duty to bring to your notice the magnificent conduct of Capt. Liddell and of Lieut Peck, both of them aviators under your command.*
>
> *These officers, who were flying in a Beardmore aeroplane, Type R.E.5, 120 h.p., were compelled to land on our aviation ground on July 31st, the pilot having been severely wounded. His right thigh was broken by bullets in an engagement with a German aeroplane. Thanks to his coolness and conspicuous energy he has saved his aeroplane, his companion and himself from the hands of the enemy, having had the incredible strength of will necessary to make a faultless landing on our camp. He has thus given us all a magnificent example of endurance, and one which deserves to be both mentioned and rewarded.*

The award of the VC was notified to him on 18 August, but septic poisoning set in and despite the amputation of his leg he succumbed on 31 August, exactly one month after his wounding. His mother was with him when he died and on 3 September his body was taken to London, and the following day interred in Basingstoke Old Cemetery in

Hampshire. Later the repatriation of bodies home was not allowed, unlike the United States.

Liddell's observer, Roland Henry Peck, was not to survive the war. On 5 March 1916, while flying with 30 Squadron in Mesopotamia (now Iraq) he was killed and has no known grave, being commemorated on the Basra Memorial.

Return to the main road (D928), and turn left towards St. Omer. The cemetery is a short distance down the road, on the right, beyond the civilian cemetery. The only parking spaces are on the left hand side of the road, requiring an interesting walk back across the road after parking!

Longuenesse (St. Omer) Souvenir Cemetery

This cemetery (No. 13) contains the remains of 113 members of the British and Commonwealth flying services – the largest number in any cemetery from the Great War. This is due to the fact that No. 1 Aircraft Depot, the very hub of the RFC for most of the war, was situated at the top of the hill. A book could be written on just this one site but I have chosen just a couple of representative casualties.

St. Omer was also the General Headquarters of the British Expeditionary Force from October 1914 until March 1916. As an important supply base it was a large hospital centre with eight stationary hospitals and four casualty clearing stations being situated here at one time or another. There are 2,874 First World War burials of which only six are unidentified. There are a great number of different nationalities and an enormous variety of headstone designs, including a number of CWGC civilian gardeners' graves.

A bomb incident (I A19)

The first grave, that of Air Mechanic First Class W G Woolridge, we are visiting is situated at the far side of the cemetery from the entrance, beyond the French graves, and against the hedge. It is the nineteenth grave from the left hand end.

On the outbreak of war the RFC was arguably the best equipped British army corps as far as motor transport was concerned. They had commandeered a motley collection of civilian vehicles, some of which retained their owner's colourful company identities. One of these was a lorry which had belonged to Maple, the well-known furniture company. On the evening of Sunday 8 November it was parked in a hangar as the roll call was being carried out, when an unknown individual threw a bomb or hand grenade at it. Air Mechanics F G Beale, E R Carr, A Grange, W Spours, W G Woolridge, and Corporal V J Callus, all of 5 Squadron, were wounded. No reason for the incident was ever discovered nor the culprit found. Woolridge died of his injuries the next day and was buried at 1500 hours on 10 November.

William George Woolridge was born in Odiham, Hampshire in 1893 and had been a motor mechanic before joining up. He was a direct entrant into the RFC, which he joined on 25 August 1913 at South Farnborough. He was promoted to air mechanic first class on 1 April 1914 and went out to France with 5 Squadron on 15 August.

All the others survived the war but Spours deserted in March 1915, rejoining in June 1917. He deserted again in July 1917, for which he forfeited his 1914 Star.

John Cowell DCM, MM and Bar (V D19)

The next grave we are paying our respects to is that of one of the most successful gunners in the RFC and arguably the most decorated. It is situated in the plot to the right of the Cross of Sacrifice. It is in the fourth row from the back and about a quarter of the way along from the left.

Most records show him as J J Cowell, but in his official papers he is shown just as John. Born in Limerick, he had been a fitter in civilian life. Before joining the RFC he had served in 12th Field Company Royal Engineers. His Military Medal was earned while a sapper/acting lance-corporal in this unit and was gazetted on 27 October 1916. On 26 March 1917 he transferred to the RFC in the rank of air mechanic second class and was posted to 20 Squadron, who were based at Ste-Marie-Cappel flying FE2s (page 186).

He claimed his first victory on 5 May 1917, when he shot down an Albatros DIII out of control while flying with Second Lieutenant R E Conder. Just three weeks later, on 26 May, he claimed his fifth machine, thus becoming an ace, although this term did not officially exist in British military circles for pilots, let alone gunners. Promotion to sergeant was promulgated on 5 June and by the end of July he had claimed fifteen enemy machines, whilst flying with five different pilots. An award of the DCM was gazetted on 21 July and a Bar to his MM on 17 September. Cowell returned to the UK for pilot training and this was conducted at 35 Training Squadron, together with a course at No. 2 School of Aerial Gunnery.

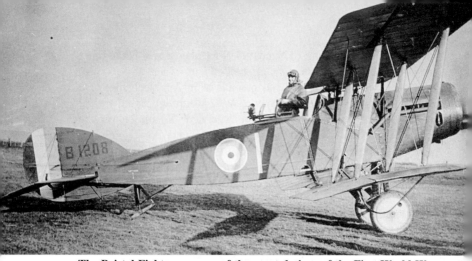

The Bristol Fighter was one of the great designs of the First World War and served the RAF for many years.

On 24 July 1918 he was posted from No. 10 Training Squadron back to his old unit, who were now at Boisdinghem. While Cowell had been away 20 Squadron had replaced their lumbering but, nonetheless, much loved FE2s with the formidable Bristol Fighter. The introduction of the Bristol had been disastrous with heavy losses (*Arras* page 172). Once it had been realised that the aeroplane should be flown aggressively as a two-seat fighter and not in the traditional manner, where everything relied on the gunner, it became a difficult opponent.

Five days later Cowell claimed his sixteenth victim, a Fokker DVII, northwest of Wervicq. Unfortunately, before he could get into his stride as a fighter pilot, he was shot down and killed. On 30 July at 1825 hours a large formation of Bristols encountered ten enemy machines at 15,000 feet north of Armentières. Attacked from the left they drove them off but then a second group of fifteen attacked the right side of the 20 Squadron formation and were soon joined by a third. A dogfight ensued, in which two enemy machines were shot down in flames, and another sent down out of control. However, two of the Bristols also went down in flames, one of them being Cowell's.

In the casualty return forwarded by the squadron to headquarters, it was noted that the observer's body had been found but not that of the pilot. They crashed just north of Bailleul, inside the British front line and, apart from going down in flames, the machine had also broken up. The wreckage was probably distributed over a large area as Cowell's observer, C W Hill, was buried initially at Mont Vidaigne but later moved to Klein-Vierstraat British Cemetery (No. 94), just south of Ypres. Cowell, however, was admitted to 58 Casualty Clearing Station (also known as West Riding CCS) at Longuenesse, dead on arrival, which is almost twenty kilometres away to the west.

Charles William Hill was born in Aston, Birmingham and was aged 23 when he enlisted in the RFC on 6 January 1915. In peacetime he had been a painter. On 1 July 1915 he was promoted to air mechanic first class and then to corporal on 1 March 1917.

Oberleutnant Friedrich Röth

Cowell and Smith almost certainly fell foul of Fritz Röth, a very experienced, seasoned ace and commander of Bavarian *Jasta* 16*b*. Born on 29 September 1893 in Nüremberg, he served with a field artillery regiment in the early part of the war but was wounded, spending nearly a year in hospital. He then transferred to the flying service and was severely injured in a flying accident, resulting in him

Friedrich Röth, victor over John Cowell.

being in hospital for yet another year. After pilot training he served in *FA(A) 296b*, a Bavarian two-seater unit. Following a spell at *jastaschule* he went to *Jasta 34b*, then on to *Jasta 23b*, also Bavarian units. In June he received the Bavarian Military Merit Order 4th Class with Swords. Finally he went to *Jasta 16b*, which he commanded until he was wounded in the foot on 14 October 1918, the day on which he scored his twenty-eighth and last victory. He had been awarded the coveted *Pour le Mérite* on 9 September, after his twenty-second claim.

The German army was mainly a Prussian one, though certain states were large enough to have their own separate units. Bavarian flying units were distinguished by the suffix *b*, Württemberg by *w* and Saxon units by the letter *s*, but all remained under overall Prussian command.

Röth was unusual as only eight of his victims were aeroplanes, with Cowell and Hill being his seventeenth victory. All the rest were kite balloons, making him the German highest scorer against these difficult and dangerous targets. Also, they were all shot down in multiples; three on 25 January 1918, two on 21 March, four on 1 April, five on 29 May, three on 13 August and three on 10 October. After the war he could not bear Germany's defeat and committed suicide on New Year's Eve 1919. He was posthumously awarded the Knight's Cross of the Military Max-Joseph Order, which entitled him to be known as Friedrich *Ritter* von Röth.

The other Bristol lost in the same engagement as Cowell and Hill was that of Lieutenant G H Zellers and his observer Sergeant J D Cormack, who were both killed. They possibly fell victim to *Leutnant* Franz Piechulek of *Jasta* 56, though there is some doubt resulting from the time of his claim. Cormack is buried in Hagle Dump Cemetery (No. 69), just east of Poperinghe. Zellers was a member of the US Air Service and is buried in Wareghem American Cemetery, northeast of Courtrai (*Ypres* page 151).

Continue down the hill, and at the traffic lights, turn right onto the St. Omer ring road, the N42. Proceed on the N42 Cassel, then the D933 Cassel. Turn left onto the D55 Clairmarais, then right on D209 Noordpeene (before the right turn, there is a large red sign bearing the number 85. On your left here was the site of Clairmarais South airfield). Continue to the sharp bends marked by sets of chevrons, and turn left D55E Clairmarais. After about 300 metres, and beyond the last farmhouse, park on the hard standing to the right of the road.

Picture No.28. Looking northwest in 2005.

Claimarais Aerodrome

Documentary evidence for this site is very sparse and based on the little information available where you are now parked is the most likely location of this historic aerodrome.

It is sometimes also referred to as Clairmarais North, and is not to be confused with Clairmarais South, which was a mile to the south. Clairmarais was a much older, well-established site with corrugated iron hangars. In official documents it is often difficult trying to decide which units were based at these aerodromes. Only one squadron, No. 74, was based at both. It was from here on 7 January 1917 that Sergeant Thomas Mottershead took off in an FE2 of 20 Squadron and earned his Victoria Cross (*Ypres* page 61).

Units stationed here at various times were 20, 27, 49, 54, 58, 65, 74, 98, 9 Naval (209 from 1 April 1918) and 4 Australian Flying Corps.

It is in this last unit that we are particularly interested. Of all the colonies or parts of the British Empire, Australia was the only one to

Sopwith Camel B2489 of 4 AFC. This was a 'Presentation Machine' having been bought from donations by the citizens of New South Wales in Australia.

Clairmarais Aerodrome

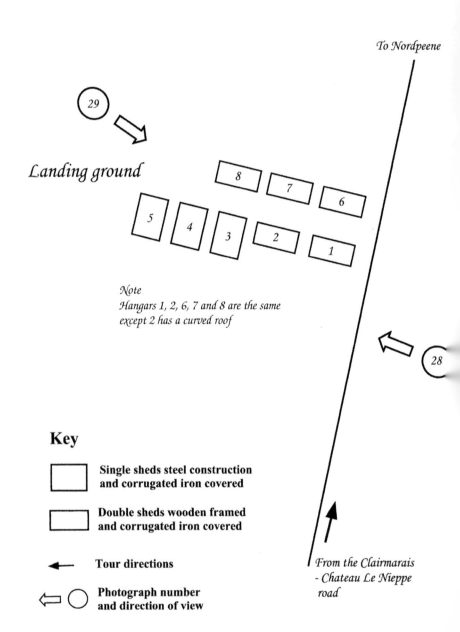

Picture No.29. Left to right, Lieutenants J H Weingarth, R G Smallwood and V G M Sheppard of 4 AFC in front of a Sopwith Camel. All three pilots survived the war.

form its own independent flying units during the First World War. The Canadians were organising their first wing when the war finished and it did not see operational service.

There were four Australian squadrons, of which three were formed in Australia. The fourth originated as part of No. 1 AFC in the Middle East and was sent to the UK. These were designated by the British as 67, 68, 69 and 71 Squadrons RFC but almost certainly the Australians used their own numbers. In January and February 1918 these RFC squadrons were disbanded and renumbered as Australian units. Thus 67 became 1 AFC, 68 re-numbered as 2 AFC, 69 as 3 AFC and lastly 71 Squadron re-mustered as 4 AFC. When the Royal Air Force was formed on 1 April 1918 from the RFC and RNAS, the AFC remained independent.

While 4 AFC was stationed here A H Cobby, the Australian Flying Corps' highest scoring ace, claimed nearly half his victories.

Arthur Henry Cobby

Born on 26 August 1894 in Melbourne, Cobby had been a bank clerk before the war. Joining the AFC at the end of 1916 he crossed to France in early January 1918 and was posted to 71 Squadron RFC. The first confirmed victory for the unit, a DFW two-seater, was shot down by Captain A H O'Hara-Wood on 24 January. He was later killed when commanding 46 Squadron (*Somme* page 163).

King George V visiting 4 AFC on 10 August 1918. He is talking to Roy King (left) and A H Cobby (right). To the right of His Majesty, with a moustache, is Major W A McClaughry, the squadron commander. On the right looking at the camera is General Birdwood, commanding Australian and New Zealand forces.

Cobby claimed his first victories on 21 March 1918, when he brought down two Albatros DVs. His early days with 4 AFC coincided with the great German offensive of spring 1918. He was an extremely aggressive but calculating pilot and in addition to his air fighting duties was heavily engaged in attacking ground targets during the enemy advance. During mid-May Cobby was promoted to flight commander and by the end of the month he had claimed a total of eight enemy machines.

His thirteenth victim, shot down on 19 June, was *Unteroffizier* Max Mertens of *Jasta* 7, who was killed. The wreckage was given the captured aeroplane number G/2 Brigade/16 and the tailskid from this machine is now in the Australian War Memorial, Canberra. Cobby's twenty-ninth and last victory, a Fokker DVII, was claimed on 4 September and he was then posted to the UK for instructional duties. On 2 July his DFC was gazetted and a Bar, plus a second Bar, were both gazetted on 21 September 1918. Shortly afterwards he was awarded a DSO.

Joining the Royal Australian Air Force after the war, he became a wing commander in 1933 but resigned during 1936 to become Controller of Operations in the Civil Aviation Board. In 1940 Cobby returned to the RAAF and by August 1942 had become commander of the RAAF in Western Australia. On 7 September 1943 he was a passenger on an aircraft which crashed, and for his actions in saving other passengers' lives, even though he was injured, he was subsequently awarded a George Medal. He retired from the air force in 1946 as an air commodore to return to civil aviation, having received a CBE. Cobby died on Armistice Day 1955, aged only 61.

Return to the D933, and turn right for St. Omer. Return to the St. Omer ring road, and turn left at the roundabout onto the N43 Bethune. Continue on the N43 to Lambres-sur-la-Lys, then turn left for Trézennes. Continue ahead over the crossroads, and take the first side road to the right, signed Stade de la Roupie. Park on the right.

Treizennes Aerodrome

This was also a busy aerodrome and a great many squadrons operated from here. The first unit to arrive was No.18 Squadron with their Vickers FB5 pusher machines on 25 October 1915. They were to spend three periods at Treizennes. Other units who utilised the aerodrome at different times were: 4, 6, 22, 27, 32, 40, 42, 43, 58, 100, 102, 203, and 210. The great ace Mick Mannock began his career at this site flying Nieuport scouts with 40 Squadron.

However the aerodrome is perhaps best associated with L W B Rees who, while commanding 32 Squadron here, earned the seventh Victoria Cross awarded to an airman.

Picture No.30. The aerodrome looking southeast in 2005.

Treizennes Aerodrome

Notes
Hangars 4, 5, 6 and 7 each have billets
at the rear holding 30 men in triple tier
bunks

Hangars 2 and 3 each have billets at the
rear holding 20 men

Hangar 1 has a billet at the rear holding
22 men

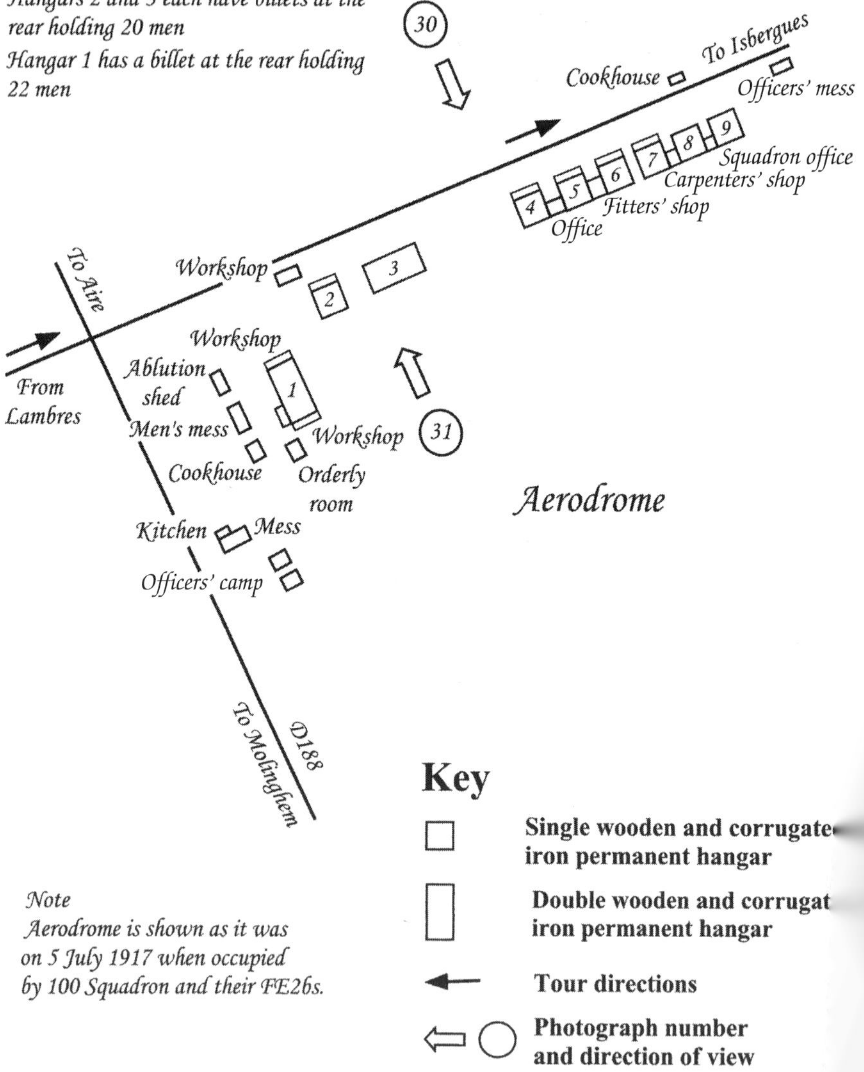

To Isbergues

Cookhouse

Officers' mess

30

Squadron office

9

8

7

Carpenters' shop

5

6

Fitters' shop

4

Office

To Aire

Workshop

3

2

Workshop

From
Lambres

Ablution
shed

1

Men's mess

Workshop

31

Cookhouse

Orderly
room

Aerodrome

Kitchen

Mess

Officers' camp

To Molinghem

D188

Key

☐   **Single wooden and corrugate
iron permanent hangar**

▯   **Double wooden and corrugat
iron permanent hangar**

◄   **Tour directions**

⇐ ◯   **Photograph number
and direction of view**

Note
Aerodrome is shown as it was
on 5 July 1917 when occupied
by 100 Squadron and their FE2bs.

Picture No.31. Nieuport Scouts of 40 Squadron in March/April 1917. The nearest machine, A6781, also flew with 1 and 29 Squadrons.

Lionel Wilmot Brabazon Rees VC

Gwilym Lewis, a junior pilot in 32 Squadron, wrote in his autobiography *Wings over the Somme*:

> Major L. W. B. Rees is in command and it is he who makes the squadron mostly ideal. He has got permission to go out as a flying squadron commander, and he can teach every member of his squadron how to fly. He has published a booklet on how to rig the DH2 and was this evening giving a lecture on the Mono engine. He knows his job thoroughly and above all is a perfect gentleman. I shouldn't be surprised if he comes home with a V.C.; he has already got an MC.

Rees was born on 31 July 1884, the son of a colonel. While attending Eastbourne College, he also decided to follow his father into the army and enrolled at the Royal Military College at Woolwich. On 23 December 1903 following commissioning, he joined the Royal Garrison Artillery. Two years were spent with the West African Frontier

L W B Rees wearing his VC and MC ribbons.

Force but in January 1907 he learned to fly, while gaining his Royal Aero Club 'ticket' No. 392. As a result of his new-found interest, on his return from West Africa he applied for a secondment to the RFC. This was granted and on 10 August 1914 the transfer took effect. He spent a short period as an instructor, before joining 11 Squadron, equipping with Vickers FB5 two-seaters at Netheravon. They were forming as the RFC's first dedicated fighting squadron. On 29 July 1915 the unit flew to France landing at Vert Galand.

Rees wasted no time in taking the war to the enemy, and his aggressive tactics soon resulted in a number of engagements with German machines. With his gunner, Sergeant J M Hargreaves, they succeeded in shooting down two enemy aeroplanes and forcing others down (*Somme* page 127). In October 1915 Rees received the MC and Hargreaves the DCM, then the following month Rees returned to the UK.

After a period of leave he was posted to No. 32 Squadron, as its commanding officer, which was forming for service in France as a single-seater fighter unit. They were to operate the DH2 and, after training, departed for France on 28 May 1916. A little over a week later they arrived at Treizennes.

During the next three weeks patrols and escort of bombing machines were carried out in preparation for the Battle of the Somme, which began on 1 July, after an unprecedented week long artillery barrage. At approximately 0600 hours two DH2s took off, one piloted by Rees and the other by J C Simpson.

Gwilym Lewis again:

> *The next day after our big raid, there being less wind, the Huns came over in one of their little bunches of eleven. J. C. Simpson, of Canada, met them and attacked them. Three detached themselves to attack. According to all trench reports he sent one of them down 'looping', then got his head in the way of a few bullets, and arrived just our side of the Lines. He was one of our cleverest DH pilots.*

> *The Major (Rees) happened to be up at the same time on a DH. I told you he was the bravest man in the world. He came across them a little later, and the archie's batteries say they have never seen anything so gallant or comic in their lives. The Huns were in a tight little bunch when he came along – after he had finished they were all scattered in twos and ones all over the sky, not knowing which way to go. He sent the first one down out of control; the second one probably had a bullet through his*

engine. He turned to attack the third, whose observer was sitting with his head back and his gun aiming vertically upwards fairly blazing off bullets. I suppose he must have forgotten to take his hand off the trigger before he 'pipped out'. Just as the Major was going to get this machine as a trophy another fellow came and shot him in the leg from below. He was still going on but discovered he couldn't steer his machine, so he came home.

He landed in the usual manner – taxied in. They got steps for him to get out of his machine. He got out and sat on the grass, and calmly told the fellows to bring him a tender to take him to hospital. I am afraid he got a very bad wound, though he is lucky not to have had an artery in his leg shot, as I understand he would never have got back if he had.

Of course, everyone knows the Major is mad. I don't think he was ever more happy in his life than attacking those Huns. He said he would have brought them all down one after the other if he could have used his leg. He swears they were youngsters on their first bombing lesson!! I don't know how he does it!

What Lewis omits to mention is that Rees, despite a bad wound, continued to pursue the leader of the enemy formation all the way back to the front line before giving up the chase.

On 5 August 1916 the announcement of a VC to Rees was made. Following a tour of the USA he was promoted to command of No. 1 School of Aerial Fighting, with the rank of lieutenant-colonel. Here his experience and example were employed in the training of the offensive spirit exemplified by his actions.

By the end of the war Rees had been awarded the OBE and AFC and in 1919 he received a permanent commission in the RAF. Various postings followed throughout the 1920s, including Assistant Commandant of the newly created RAF College at Cranwell and command of RAF Headquarters Transjordan.

In 1931 he retired and two years later sailed solo across the Atlantic to Nassau in the Bahamas. This feat was rewarded by the Cruising Club of America's Blue Water Medal. He spent much of the 1930s cruising round the Bahamas but in 1940 rejoined the RAF, dropping a rank from group captain to wing commander. Serving in the Middle East and West Africa, he returned to civilian life in 1942. Returning to the Bahamas, he eventually set up a tiny farm on the island of Andros. He employed an eighteen year old black housekeeper, Sylvia Williams, and shortly they became emotionally involved. When she became pregnant Rees, as an officer and gentleman, did the honourable thing and married her. This scandalised white Bahamian society, and it was predicted that the marriage would not last.

Rees, in anticipation of the happy event built a single-roomed house of corrugated iron. In March 1948 a son was born and over the next few years there were two more children. Contrary to predictions, the marriage was a happy one and Rees revelled in teaching his eldest son all he knew. Unfortunately the idyll was not to last, as in the early 1950s he was diagnosed with leukaemia and on 28 September 1955 died in hospital at Nassau.

Despite the fact he was not a wartime casualty, permission was given for him to be buried in the Commonwealth War Graves cemetery in Nassau and, as is the custom in hot climates, the funeral was the same day.

Curiously for such an amazing person and a famous VC holder, there has only been one book written about him. This is *Against the Odds* by W Alister Williams (see the Further Reading Section).

Mind that horse!

Two other individuals, who were to reach the pinnacles of their professions, served at Treizennes, both in 43 Squadron. One was Harold Balfour, one of the flight commanders, who later became Under Secretary of State for Air and finished his career as Lord Balfour of Inchrye. For some years he was President of *Cross and Cockade*.

The other was W S Sholto-Douglas, the squadron commander who, in the fullness of time and a distinguished career, reached the rank of Marshal of the Royal Air Force. Sholto-Douglas commanded 43 Squadron from April 1916 until May 1917 operating the obsolete Sopwith 1¹/₂ Strutter and had a difficult time, with serious losses.

No. 43 Squadron was formed at Montrose on 15 April 1916 from a nucleus of 18 Reserve Squadron. On 17 January 1917 they crossed to St. Omer and eight days later to their permanent home at Treizennes.

On 7 May Douglas was watching one of his flights departing on patrol, when the leader suffered an engine failure and landed in a field adjacent to the aerodrome. Unfortunately, this left the formation under the command of an inexperienced deputy leader. Jumping into his machine, accompanied by his observer, Douglas took off in a violent hurry to take over, omitting to do up his safety belt.

What happened next he related in his book *Years of Combat*:

> As I tore off across the field I did not notice what I was later told was a large white horse at work with a plough in the

adjoining field right in my line of take off. I held the nose of my aircraft down so as to be able to zoom up after my squadron, but just as I was clear of the ground I hit the unfortunate plough-horse slap on its backside with my under-carriage, and we crashed beyond it, upside down, in the ploughed field. It was fortunate for me that I was thrown clear, through not having done up my safety-harness, because the engine was slammed back into the pilot's seat, and I shudder to think what would have happened to me if I had been strapped in. My poor observer was thrown clear, landing on his head in the plough; and was promptly taken off to hospital.

When they collected me it was found that I was concussed, that my nose was bent across my face, and that I had received a hard bash in one eye, which was already swelling. I flatly refused to go to hospital, and I spent the next twenty-four hours in bed in my hut, all of it in considerable pain. Then Wilfred Freeman came to see me, and apparently I babbled such nonsense to him that he immediately ordered that I should be whisked off to hospital without further delay. Later he told me about the nonsense that I had talked, and it was the sort of thing that appealed to his sense of humour.

Freeman was Douglas' wing commander and eventually retired as Air Chief Marshal Sir Wilfred, GCB, DSO, MC. His brother was killed whilst flying with the RAF in 1918 (*Airfields and Airmen: Verdun*, Raperie British Cemetery).

Douglas was invalided home but returned later in command of 84 Squadron (*Cambrai* page 120). He concludes the story:

I was not to visit the airfield at Treizennes again, although I saw it often enough from the air during the rest of the war, until forty-two years later. It took some finding when I went in search of it on my tour of the old Western Front in the spring of 1959, but after careful searching I finally recognised the field not far from the outskirts of the old town of Aire, which stands beside the River Lys. Aire had been a fortress in the centuries gone by, and it was busy with a British Army Headquarters at the time I was flying from Treizennes in 1917; but in 1959 it was a quiet country town lying in a highly cultivated but dull countryside.

The field that we had used for our flying in 1917 was in appearance exactly as it had been before, and after he had taken a few photographs Bob Wright called to my attention something we had not noticed but which he was seeing through the view-

finder of his camera. For all the mechanisation in agriculture of to-day, the ploughing of the field that was in progress as we watched it was still being done by horses, and fine big white horses at that.

'I wonder how many generations separate those from the one you knocked out?' Wright asked.

At the road turn right, continue to the next crossroads, and turn right onto the D187 Isbergues Centre. At the traffic lights turn left D186 Calonne sur la Lys. Cross the D916, then left Calonne sur la Lys. Continue to Calonne, and in the village go straight ahead onto the D180. At the first crossroad turn right into Rue de Poncelet. Stop just beyond the first track on the right (Site 1). Proceed a further 100 yards and stop (Site 2). Proceed beyond the track on to your right and on the right hand corner the area to the right is Site 3. Continue to the main road and turn left (Rue de Calonne) and at the T-junction turn left (Rue de Cornet Malo). Shortly after take the first right and on a double bend stop and the area of the Mannock crash is between you and Pacaut Wood (Site 4).

Pacaut Wood

There has been considerable controversy in recent years regarding the position of Mick Mannock's crash site and possible burial place on 26 July 1918. For an account of his career see *Ypres* page 106 and for the circumstances of his death, *Arras* page 38.

A number of people saw Mannock crash, not only D C Inglis, who was his pupil that day, but also a number of British ground observers,

Picture No. 32. Pacaut Wood and Butter Lane looking north in 2005.

Pacaut Wood

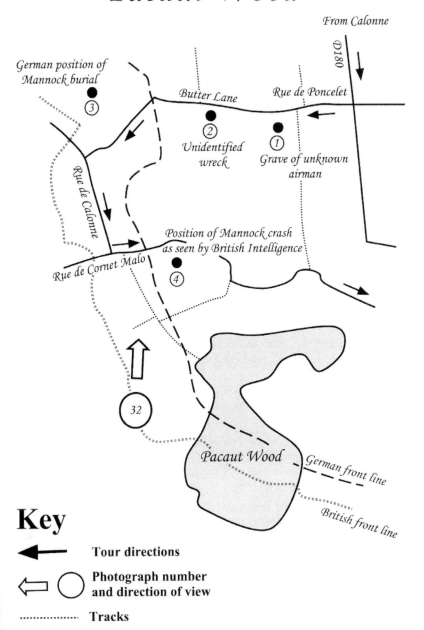

From Calonne

D180

German position of
Mannock burial

● ③

Butter Lane

Rue de Poncelet

● ②

Unidentified
wreck

● ①

Grave of unknown
airman

Rue de Calonne

Position of Mannock crash
as seen by British Intelligence

Rue de Cornet Malo

● ④

32

Pacaut Wood

German front line

British front line

Key

⬅ **Tour directions**

⇐ ◯ **Photograph number
and direction of view**

·········· **Tracks**

including Private Edward Naulls of 2/Essex Regiment. In 1919 Jim Eyles, Mannock's great friend, instituted enquiries with the Imperial War Graves Commission (as it was then). In response to Eyles' persistence the IWGC office in Berlin found during 1921 a German report which said that Mannock... *crashed in flames. Body recovered and buried at a point 300m north-west of la Pierre au Beure on the road to Pacaut* (see site 3 on the Pacaut map). This single piece of information has generated an entire industry attempting to interpret its significance. Unfortunately, by this time battlefield clearance and the collection of isolated graves had virtually finished and any clues would long ago have been ploughed back into the ground or been removed by farmers reclaiming their land.

The War Graves Commission searched the records of the nearest cemeteries to see if there was a burial that matched the location of the original grave, but failed to find one. Pressed further they then searched for any graves that had been found in the area. South of Butter Lane an unknown British airman had been discovered buried next to the remains of his machine (see site 1 on the map) and further west a second unidentified wreck had been located (see site 2 on the map). Another factor which further complicated the issue is that la Pierre au Beure is an area and not a village. The unidentified airman from Butter Lane was re-interred in grave F12, Plot III at Laventie.

Since the last correspondence between Jim Eyles and the IWGC in 1924, various people have tried to link the three pieces of information; the German message, the unknown airman and the other crash, in order to prove Mannock's actual burial site. The first published attempt to make the facts fit the story was with the publication of *Mick*, a biography of Mannock by James Dudgeon in 1981. The excellent video *Where They Flew and Where They Fell* in 1990, though not actually entirely agreeing with the theory, did not actually disprove it either. Even I, with the publication of *Airfields and Airmen: Ypres*, happily went along with the Laventie story. With the passage of time and repetition, it has become almost accepted that the unknown airman at Laventie is Mannock.

What is now Plot III at Laventie contains the overflow from the original cemetery, and virtually all the graves are interred in chronological order. Row F is completely chronological, with the first burial being 25 February 1917 and the last 28 April 1917. Our unknown airman is halfway along this line. After the German offensive of spring 1918, when the area was captured, there were no more British burials until it was re-taken by the Allies in September. Though there may have been a gap in the 1917 Row F, which could have been filled with a 1918 casualty, this is exceedingly unlikely. The evidence strongly suggests that grave F12 was a 1917 burial.

In the late 1980s Les Cook, a Mannock researcher, found a 12 Brigade Intelligence summary which described the crash and confirms the eye-witness account of Private Naulls used by Dudgeon in his book. This places the crash well south of the original position and makes a complete nonsense of the German message of 1921 (see site 4 on the map).

Mick Mannock.

So what did happen to Mannock's body? After the passage of nearly ninety years and the destruction of the records associated with the teams involved in the battlefield clearance, it is impossible to say, and anything else is pure speculation. From the evidence available the body in grave F12, Plot III at Laventie is not Mannock. All that can be said is that Major Edward Mannock VC is still missing.

For a complete account I would recommend *Major Mannock and the Laventie Myth* by Chris Page in *Cross and Cockade International* Volume 35, page 121.

Continue ahead through Le Pacault and at the D180 turn left then immediate right down Rue de Paradis through Le Paradis and at the crossroads turn right on the GC 178 (D178) to Béthune. Go straight ahead to the D945. At the D945 turn left to La Couture and continue into Estaires. Pick up signs for the D947. Proceed northwards on the D947 to Caestre, then turn left at the roundabout onto the D933 Steenvoorde. Continue ahead on D933 St. Sylvestre Cappel, going ahead at the roundabout for D916 Cassel. Turn left onto D53 Ste-Marie-Cappel. Drive through the village and past the church. Continue out of the village, and after leaving the village limits take the second right turn (the first is marked by chevrons) into Campagne Dreve. Continue down the lane to the farm.

Ste-Marie-Cappel

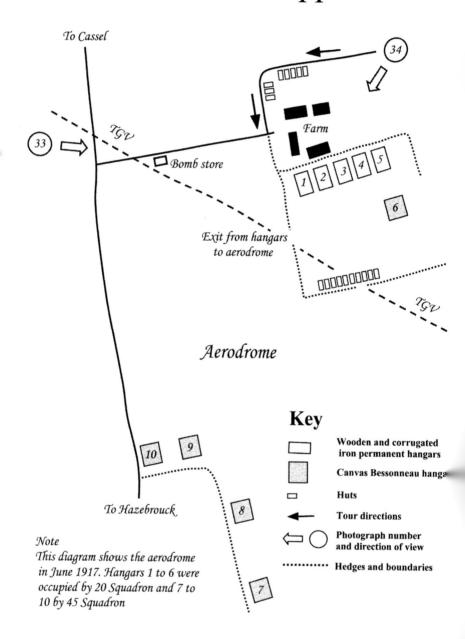

To Cassel

34

TGV

33

Bomb store

Farm

1 2 3 4 5

6

Exit from hangars
to aerodrome

TGV

Aerodrome

10   9

Key

☐ Wooden and corrugated
   iron permanent hangars

▨ Canvas Bessonneau hanga

▭ Huts

← Tour directions

⇐ ◯ Photograph number
       and direction of view

········· Hedges and boundaries

To Hazebrouck

8

7

Note
This diagram shows the aerodrome
in June 1917. Hangars 1 to 6 were
occupied by 20 Squadron and 7 to
10 by 45 Squadron

Picture No.33. Looking east in 2002.

Ste-Marie-Cappel Aerodrome

This spot is significant in that two famous squadrons were based here, 20 and 45. It was first occupied on 4 December 1916 by 45 and lastly by the cadre of 35 Squadron who departed on 3 March 1919. Other units in occupation between those dates were 1, 4, 19, 20, 46, 48, 53, 57, 60, 79, 1 Naval (201), 6 Naval (206) and 210.

Norman Macmillan, a pilot in 45 Squadron and later a distinguished test pilot and author, described the aerodrome in his book *Into the Blue*:

> *Ste Marie Cappel airfield lay on the flat farm land of the plain of Flanders, where even small hills assumed the importance of mountains.*
>
> *The aerodrome was a square field bounded by two roads, three ditches, a row of trees, a hedge partly obscuring camouflaged hangars, a farm and its poplar-lined paddock. A narrow and rough-surfaced overshoot projected from the south-east of the square. Some obstruction had to be avoided on every approach.*
>
> *The squadron's aircraft were housed in sheds. Our sleeping quarters were Nissen huts. The mess was built of wood. Its smallness, in size and the number of its inmates, made for closer companionship than had been possible at Upavon's larger mess.*

187

Picture No.34. Looking south in 1916.

Neither radio broadcasting nor television existed. The only available form of recorded entertainment was the clockwork gramophone and its fast-speed discs. When the mood was upon them, members of the mess preferred to make their own entertainment. Selby, an observer, was an excellent impromptu pianist. There was a violinist of some talent. Solomon, the only Jewish pilot who flew with 45 Squadron in WW1, was a skilful exponent of the one-string fiddle – the jamboogoo, we called it. These three musicians were a wonderful uplift to the spirit. When they ran through the melodious score of the current popular Chu Chin Chow, one thought of Oscar Asche and Lily Brayton, Ali Baba and the Forty Thieves, and forgot the war. When they played the popular songs of the day they were accompanied by a rousing chorus of masculine voices of varied melodic charm. Some notes from the jamboogoo pained one's ears; then someone (perhaps Solomon himself) would stuff a rag into its horn to mute the fervour of its vibrating string.

The Sopwith 1½ Strutters of 'C' Flight 45 Squadron with either Mont Cassel or Mont des Recollets in the background.

In early 1917 No. 45 Squadron needed all the uplifting they could get as they were equipped with the Sopwith 1½ Strutter which was employed on tasks totally unsuited for it and, as a consequence, they suffered appalling and unnecessary casualties.

Frank Courtney, a flight commander in 45 Squadron, and subsequently, like Norman Macmillan, a famous test pilot, wrote in his book *Flight Path*:

> *No. 45 Squadron had come out from England with its Sopwith fighters barely two months previously. But it had already taken such a beating that it was back at a 'rest' area in Boisdinghem for refitting and for more crew training in the techniques of the new two-seater type of fighting that this plane was supposed to conduct. Nobody considered, at the time, that the squadron's troubles had been due to anything much worse than inexperience plus, perhaps, an overdose of bad luck.*

> *Before long, however, we were going to find out, at heavy cost, that we were up against more drastic difficulties than mere inexperience, and we were due to compile such a record of losses that we would earn the title of 'The Suicide Club'.*

> *After a few weeks of refitting and what we hoped was suitable training, No.45 Squadron left Boisdinghem to return to the fighting front. Our field was a large piece of farmland at Ste. Marie Capelle (sic), a few miles south of Hazebrouck. We were in trouble from the start, and we got deeper into it as we went along.*

45 Squadron's tented accommodation with a canvas Bessonneau in the background.

The early Fokkers had now been replaced by a new crop of German fighters, twin-gunned and demonstrating performances with which they could literally run rings around us. For a short while, as long as we had enough practiced crews, we could hit back at these enemies with gratifying effect, and they showed their respect for us by their reluctance to attack unless they substantially outnumbered us. But, as our old hands were gradually picked off, to be replaced by newcomers with less and less training and experience, the going began to get progressively tougher.

Our really serious troubles started early in the game, when the Staff began to load upon us other duties, which these chair-borne gentlemen apparently supposed would be merely incidental to our fighting.

The Staff decided that, instead of using us as fighter protection for regular photographic planes, we should do both the fighting and the photography ourselves. After all, said the Staff, there was plenty of room in the gunner's cockpit for a camera installation, and he ought to have plenty of time between fights to take photos. Worse still - from our standpoint – our Sopwiths had come to us with the long range capacity that the Navy had required of them for long overwater patrols, and we had about five hours' fuel instead of the usual 2½ – 3 hours' supply. This encouraged the Staff to send us out farther and keep us out longer, for photographic purposes.

We became used to losing two out of three planes or three out of eight, and there were occasions when we wondered how any of us got back at all.

To have survived those tough months in No. 45 I needed a heavy overdraft on my brimming store of luck. But this sort of luck could not go on forever, and, like most of us now my early eagerness for battle had worn very thin.

One day the Brigadier – who had never himself flown in any serious action – visited the squadron and broadcast some ill-timed comments that implied we were not using our planes to best effect. I replied with some undiluted remarks concerning the Brigade's directives. A few days later I was sent home, and I have to admit that I was not inclined to dispute the sentence – if that's what it was.

The squadron began replacing the 1½ Strutters with Sopwith Camels in July 1917 and the last of them left at the beginning of September.

An FE2 of 20 Squadron.

During its two-seater period from October 1916 until September 1917, 45 Squadron lost sixty-four aircrew members killed in action, accidents, died of wounds or missing. A further nineteen were wounded and six more taken prisoner. And their reward for these terrible losses? Just three MCs and a single DCM.

Norman Macmillan again:

> *No.45 Squadron received orders to prepare another squadron site at Ste Marie Cappel airfield. A position diagonally opposite was inspected and approved. Four Bessoneux wood-frame, canvas-covered hangars were delivered and erected, squadron headquarters and photographic huts built, hardstands for workshop lorries and transport made with pit-props. Each operational flight's mess was in a marquee; the squadron headquarters flight mess had to make shift with an army bell tent. When all was ready, 45 Squadron was told to move over, and 20 Squadron, being senior to 45, was given our former quarters. Its transport drove in the day we moved and a day later, on 16 April 1917, its FE2d pushers landed from Boisdinghem.*
>
> *We were not overjoyed at being turned out of warm huts and sheds in mid-April of a cold spring to work, live and sleep under canvas, without even floorboards to cover the sodden grass that soon became mud under our trampling feet. If 20 Squadron had not proved to be the magnificent squadron it was on its pusher biplanes and, in the autumn, on Bristol Fighters, we should*

never have forgiven them. As it was, our chagrin was short-lived, and soon we were proud to share the airfield and co-operate with 20 across the lines when our patrols met, or worked together as they sometimes did.

Return to the D916 and turn right to St-Sylvestre-Cappel. After the village, turn left at the roundabout onto the D37 Steenvoorde. Approaching Steenvoorde, turn left for Steenvoorde Centre Ville, and in the centre of the village pick up the D947 Bray-Dunes. Continue over the motorway, and in Droogland continue ahead on the D947. At the second right turn (marked by five poplar trees) turn right. Park on the right. The airfield is on your right.

Droglandt Aerodrome

This was another old established aerodrome with the first RFC unit, a detachment of No.6 Squadron, arriving on 24 April 1915. Other units stationed here were 5, 7, 10, 15, 21, 28, 32, 41, 46, 57, 65, 70, 82 and 10 Naval. The French also had an aerodrome at Droglandt but whether they shared the site with the RFC or theirs was a completely different location is not known.

Our interest centres on two of the most successful fighter pilots of the Great War, Raymond Collishaw and William Barker, both Canadians, but one navy and the other army.

Picture No.35. The aerodrome looking north in 2005.

Droglandt Aerodrome

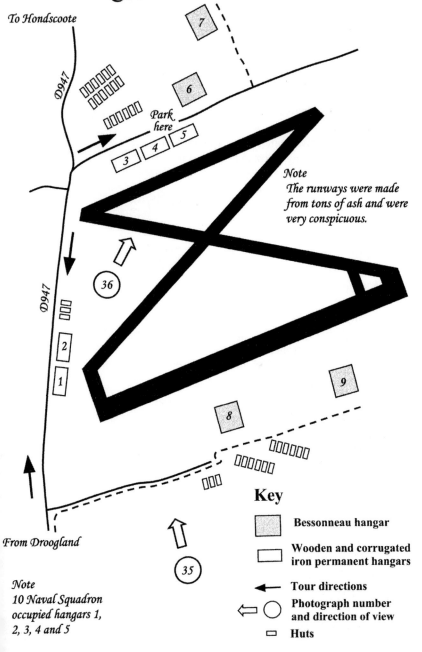

To Hondscoote

D947

7

6

Park here

5

4

3

Note
The runways were made
from tons of ash and were
very conspicuous.

D947

36

2

1

9

8

From Droogland

35

Note
10 Naval Squadron
occupied hangars 1,
2, 3, 4 and 5

Key

Bessonneau hangar

Wooden and corrugated
iron permanent hangars

Tour directions

Photograph number
and direction of view

Huts

Raymond Collishaw

Collishaw was the third most successful fighter pilot in the British and Empire flying services after Billy Bishop and Mick Mannock and the highest scoring RNAS ace.

Born on 22 November 1893 in Nanaimo, British Columbia, he joined the mercantile marine after leaving school. Joining the RNAS in January 1916, he was initially posted to 3 Wing, who were operating Sopwith 1½ Strutters bombing German targets on the French part of the front. In February 1917 he was posted to 3 Naval, who were flying Sopwith Pups. Claiming two victories with this unit, he then joined the newly-formed 10 Naval in April. This involved yet another change of type as they were equipped with the Sopwith Triplane. Claiming four more enemy machines in April and May, he and the rest of the squadron were transferred to Droglandt.

Ray Collishaw.

Collishaw described the aerodrome in his autobiography *Air Command*:

> We had known all along that Naval Ten was going to be detached to the RFC and finally the orders came through. We shifted to a new aerodrome, Droglandt, on May 14 and the following day came under the control of the RFC's 11th (Army) Wing. I flew my last patrol from Furnes the early morning of the 14th, a 2½-hour affair during which I had an indecisive scrap with a German fighter over Zarren, and later in the day led a flight of five Triplanes over to our new field. Droglandt, which was in the Second Army area, was situated 13 or 14 miles

Picture No.36. The Sopwith Triplanes of 10 Naval at Droglandt.

directly behind Ypres and so far as I know it was unique amongst our airfields on the Western Front at that time inasmuch as it had a number of runways, necessitated by the low-lying soggy ground. These runways were surfaced with rolled cinders and were laid out in the form of a St. Andrews Cross with the four corners connected in rectangular manner.

Collishaw was the principal exponent of the Triplane and subsequently became the most successful pilot of the type with thirty-four of his sixty victories being claimed on this machine. The Triplanes under his command were called the Black Flight, as they all had black-painted wheels and engine cowlings and were given individual names, with his machine being christened Black Maria. The Sopwith Triplane, with its great agility and climb rate, was a surprise to the Germans and inspired them to produce their own version, the Fokker Dr1.

His first victory while based at Droglandt was on 1 June 1917 when he shot down an Albatros DIII in flames. Collishaw claimed a further twenty-nine victories before he was posted from 10 Naval on 28 July for leave in Canada. Shortly before he left he was awarded the DSC and during his leave received the DSO.

While with 10 Naval he had an incident which could have cost him his life and cut short a promising career. It demonstrates how important good luck is for survival, especially in the days before parachutes.

We continued our patrols during the next few days without let-up but although we had plenty of scraps none of us was able to make any decisive claims. It was during one of these combats that I underwent an experience that left me somewhat shaken. We had become involved in the usual sort of dogfight, with everyone circling around trying to get one of the enemy in his sights and at the same time keeping a lookout behind to see what in turn may be on his tail. I was in exactly this position, keeping one eye on an enemy fighter in front of me and, thanks to the manoeuvrability of my Triplane, slightly more than matching the tight turns that he was making, and keeping the other eye on another enemy machine that had been trying to position itself on my tail. Things were going very well, and I almost had the German ahead of me in my sights when suddenly a third enemy machine appeared dead in front, coming straight at me. There was no time to consider stress limits and the amount of abuse the Triplane would take – I jammed my stick right forward and just passed under the German fighter. The Triplane held together in one piece but my manoeuvre had been so violent that my safety strap, holding me down in my seat, snapped. I suddenly found myself completely clear of the cockpit and instinctively grabbed at the two centre section struts just in front of the pilot's position. The control column was left to its own devices and with full power on the Triplane nosed down in a steep dive. Left to itself, under full power, the Triplane executed a series of extraordinary manoeuvres, suddenly nosing up only to drop off into a falling leaf spin and then going again into a steep dive. To anyone who might have seen me I must have presented a comic sight, clinging desperately to the two struts with the lower part of my body trailing in the slipstream and being flung about like a rag doll as my pilotless Triplane displayed its varied repertoire. So far as I was concerned, though, there was nothing funny about it at all. There was absolutely nothing that I could do, for it took all my strength merely to hang on, and I could feel my grip weakening as excruciating pains shot through my arms. It seemed only a question of whether I should be able to hang on until the aircraft and I hit the ground together or whether we would part company before then. There was always the chance that the Triplane would shed its wings but these matters seemed academic for I was apparently done for whatever happened. Had things gone on like this for only a few more moments I think that the Triplane and I would have gone our separate ways for my arms were nearly being pulled from their sockets and were starting to slip from the struts. I recall feeling almost piqued because no one seemed to notice what was happening to me and apparently no one cared. What rescue action the other members of the flight could have taken, even had they seen my predicament, is questionable, but in a situation such as I was in one is not always either logical or reasonable. Suddenly, though, the Triplane took it in its head to pull straight up sharply and the lower part of my body was slammed down on the cockpit coaming. Still hanging on, I was able to work one leg into the cockpit and hook my foot round the upper part of the control column, pulling it back until I was in more or less level flight. Then I was able to let go and regain my seat, which seemed a very secure spot indeed. As I grasped the control column both my arms felt as if they were going to drop off but I uttered no complaints. Checking my altimeter, I saw that it read under 6,000 feet. We had been above 16,000 when we began our scrap and I had fallen nearly two miles. As soon as I was able to collect my wits I set course for home, a more sober and more thoughtful pilot than I had been some moments before.

Collishaw returned from Canadian leave in November 1917 and was posted to the Seaplane Defence Squadron at St. Pol which, despite its title, was now operating Sopwith Camels. In January 1918 this became 13 Naval and after a serious accident to the commanding officer, Ronnie Graham, Collishaw was promoted to lead it. While with them he claimed two German machines, but later in the month was sent to 3 Naval as commanding officer. Due to administrative duties his flying was severely curtailed and it was to be June before he was able to get back into the air.

He then claimed another nineteen victories before being returned to the UK on 1 October 1918, finishing the war with a total of fifty-nine. In August he had received the DFC and in September a Bar to his DSO. In 1919 he commanded 47 Squadron in Russia where he shot down a Bolshevik aeroplane and received the OBE and three Czarist awards.

Remaining in the RAF post-war he held a variety of posts both afloat and ashore. During 1940 and 1941 he commanded 202 Group in the Western Desert. Returning to the UK and promoted to air vice-marshal, he commanded 14 Group. On 27 October 1943 he retired, but was retained as regional air liaison officer to the civil defence organisation. At the end of the war he and his family returned to Canada and he then went into the mining industry. Ray Collishaw died in 1976.

William George Barker

Another great Canadian ace and Victoria Cross recipient started his fighting career at Droglandt, claiming the first three of a total of fifty victories.

Barker was born on 3 November 1894 in Dauphin, Manitoba. His outdoor upbringing ensured he was an excellent horseman and shot. In November 1914 he enlisted in the Canadian Mounted Rifles where, because of his experience with rifle and pistol, he was attached to the machine gun section. In the spring of 1915 the unit sailed for the UK and initially were based in Kent, but in September crossed the Channel to the Western Front. Barker, by now a corporal, had already had one application to transfer to the RFC rejected while in the UK, and when in France applied again. This time he was successful and was attached to 9 Squadron as an NCO observer. They were flying BE2cs and, despite the cramped forward observer's cockpit, he was able to shoot down a Fokker *Eindecker* in early 1916. Commissioned in April he was posted to 4 Squadron and then in July joined 15 Squadron. While with them he managed to drive down two more German machines. For his long period as an observer, and gallantry he was awarded an MC in January 1917. His application for pilot training was approved and in November 1916 he returned to the UK.

William George Barker (right).

Amazingly, he went solo after only 55 minutes of dual instruction and, after more tuition at Netheravon, he returned to his old squadron, No. 15, at Lealvillers, down on the Somme, where he was made C Flight Commander. Barker was constantly in the air and on 23 March 1917 he drove down another Fokker but on 7 August was wounded, having been in France for six months. For courage and hard work during his second tour in 15 Squadron, he was awarded a Bar to his MC.

To his dismay he was sent as an instructor to the UK and immediately started making himself a nuisance in order to return to action. Eventually, he was given the choice of a posting to 56 Squadron or to 28 who were working up for service in France. He chose the latter, as they had the more manoeuvrable Camel and thus he was posted to 28 Squadron at Yatesbury on 2 October 1917. Appointed to command A Flight, he accompanied the unit to St. Omer six days later. As with most squadrons their tenure at the depot was brief and on 10 October they moved to Droglandt.

While leading three inexperienced members of his flight on a familiarisation patrol he shot down an Albatros scout but did not submit a claim for it as his actions had been contrary to squadron orders.

His first official claim (and for the squadron as well), was made on 20 October, when he shot the wings off an Albatros scout near Roulers. Six days later he claimed two more, one of which went down in flames. However, things were going badly on the Italian Front and the British government agreed to Italian requests for reinforcements. These consisted of six infantry divisions and six RFC squadrons.

On 29 October 1917 No.28 Squadron left Droglandt and two weeks later were in Milan. Barker continued as he had left off in France and attacked everything, including strafing ground targets and balloons. By the end of December he had claimed seven victories and three months later had a total of twenty-two, having received the DSO. Due to a disagreement with higher authority, he affected a swap with a flight commander in 66 Squadron, one of the other units on the Italian Front, and took his Camel with him. He claimed another sixteen Austro-Hungarian machines with this squadron, being awarded a second Bar to his MC, the French *Croix de Guerre* and a Mention in Despatches.

On 14 July 1918 Barker was promoted to major and took command of 139 Squadron, which had just been formed. Though they were flying Bristol Fighters he was permitted to retain his Camel. On 9 August he landed an agent behind enemy lines for which the Italians awarded him their Silver Medal for Military Valour. He claimed eight victories with 139 Squadron and received a Bar to his DSO. On 30 September, after a year on operations, Barker was posted back to the UK, having claimed forty-six victories, all but three while in Italy. His entire victory total had been claimed flying a single Camel, B6313, and he had flown an unprecedented 379 hours and 25 minutes in it. This historic machine was dismantled on 2 October 1918 as being war-weary and time-expired, but Barker was not allowed a single souvenir from it. In terms of numbers of aeroplanes shot down it was the most successful fighter in the history of the Royal Air Force.

Barker had barely finished his leave before he was agitating to return to action. Eventually, he was allowed a brief period attached to an operational squadron as a 'refresher'. Consequently, on 17 October, just three weeks after his return from Italy, he flew a Sopwith Snipe to join 201 Squadron (the old 1 Naval) at La Targette, southeast of Cambrai. Over the next ten days Barker was unable to claim an enemy machine and so, on 27 October, he packed his kit for the return flight

Barker (left) in front of his famous Camel B6313. Note the 28 Squadron marking of a white square on the top right wing.

to England. Unable to resist a last look at the lines, he spotted an enemy two-seater at 21,000 feet over the Forest of Mormal. Closing on it, he killed the observer with his first burst and then the machine broke up, ejecting the pilot who descended by parachute. Unfortunately, while involved in this action Barker allowed himself to be surprised by a large number of Fokker DVIIs, one of which wounded him in the right thigh. He dived on this machine and sent it down in flames but was then surrounded by the rest. Firing short bursts as best he could in the swirling dogfight he was hit in the left thigh, causing him to faint. Regaining consciousness he sent another DVII down before being hit in the left elbow. Barker now had minimal control of his aeroplane and eventually crash landed near 29 Kite Balloon Section, where his machine turned over.

Unconscious for several days, surgeons saved his left arm. For his action he was awarded the Victoria Cross, which he received at an investiture on 1 March 1919.

On 29 April Barker resigned his commission, as a career in the post-war RAF did not appeal. He went into the aviation business with Billy Bishop VC (*Arras* page 142) but the venture soon failed. After a short spell in the Canadian Air Force and the tobacco business, he was appointed Vice-President of Fairchild Aviation Corporation of Canada in January 1930. His new career was not to last long as on 12 March 1930 he was killed flying a new Fairchild design at Rockcliffe, Ottowa. At his funeral three days later it was estimated that there were 50,000 mourners.

Barker was interred in Mount Pleasant Cemetery, Toronto where his remains are in the crypt of his wife's family. On the outside there is no clue to the fact his body lies here. It is a great pity that to the majority of Canadians their most decorated hero is largely forgotten. Very little has been written about him but in 1997 an excellent biography, entitled *Barker VC* was published, written by a Canadian, Wayne Ralph (see Further Reading section).

Return to the main road and turn left. Take the next road on the left, the D137 to Watou. In Watou pick up signs for Poperinge. Approaching Poperinge turn right at the roundabout N308 Poperinge, then at the next junction turn right onto the ring road, R33 Andere Richtingen. Follow the ring road, and take the next right turn, following the green CWGC sign for Nine Elms Cemetery along the road to the cemetery on the left.

Nine Elms British Cemetery

There are two Nine Elms cemeteries cared for by the CWGC, but the other is situated much further south, near Arras. This one (No. 71) was first used in late 1917 by the 3rd Australian and 44th Casualty Clearing Stations. These units had been moved to the area in anticipation of the Third Battle of Ypres, which commenced in July 1917. It was employed again from March to October 1918. There are 1,556 burials from the Great War, plus thirty-seven German and twenty-four British from the fighting of 1940.

The graves we are visiting, Kurt Anders (21) and Hans Wenner (22), are in the German plot on the left as you enter the cemetery and on the right hand end of the back row. This section contains the graves of prisoners of war who died of their injuries.

The *Schlastas*

These two casualties are from a German unit which was employed specifically on ground attack duties, harassing Allied troops and artillery. In the German air service the crew of a two-seater machine were affectionately nicknamed *Emil* and *Franz*. Like many terms and expressions the origin of these names has been lost. The survival of a two-seat crew with *Emil*, the pilot and *Franz*, the observer, depended on the way they worked together, as it did on the Allied side.

The German ground support units were highly successful during the German counter-attacks mounted in the Battle of Cambrai in late 1917. The British did not have such specialised units and, when needed, employed unsuitable types in a stop gap role. RFC/RAF losses during the March 1918 German offensive were severe, with types such as the SE5a and Camel being brought down in large numbers by ground fire.

At the beginning of the First World War the German air service or *Fliegertruppe* was much larger and more developed than the RFC or RNAS. This was mainly due to the fact that the Germans had expanded their aviation element based on the development of the French flying services, which they saw as a serious threat. The very small RFC was still trying to demonstrate to the British army that it had a future in the military structure. The Germans already had a system of training observers whereas the RFC employed pilots in this role.

At the outbreak of war there were thirty-three *Feldflieger Abteilungen* or field aviation units. By the end of 1915 this figure had risen to eighty and there had been a reorganisation, in that some of these units were now dedicated to artillery cooperation. During the winter of 1915/1916 there was a further expansion when five *Kampfgeschwader der Obersten Heeresleitung (Kagohl)*, each of six *Kampfstaffeln (Kastas)* were formed. These units were directly under the control of the German High Command, rather than army or corps commanders. Unfortunately during the Verdun offensive of early 1916 in which the French rapidly regained command of the air, the *Kastas* were used in a non-strategic or defensive way and suffered heavy losses.

In the light of experience gained during the Verdun and the Somme, there was a complete reorganisation of the German air service in late 1916, including both command structure and the tasks for the various units. The *Kagohls* were reduced from three to two and were completely equipped with twin-engined machines, in order to concentrate on strategic bombing. The two-seater machine *Kastas* left were grouped together and formed thirty units, which were re-designated *Schutzstaffeln (Schustas)*.

The old *Feldflieger Abteilungen* were split into two, with the long range high altitude reconnaissance role performed by *Flieger Abteilungen* and the infantry cooperation and artillery registration by *Flieger Abteilungen (A)*. The *FA* and *FA (A)* structure was to remain in place until the end of the war. Also at this time the Germans introduced dedicated fighter units or *Jagdstaffeln (Jastas)* and their development is described in *Cambrai* page 160.

The *Schustas* initial role was to protect the *Flieger Abteilungen (A)* machines though they could be brought in on a local basis to carry out the same duties as the *FA (A)* units. However, with an increase in numbers of *FA (A)* units in late 1917 and a requirement for more support of attacking German infantry, the *Schustas* could be released from escort duties. Their main task now was attacking enemy targets on the ground with machine guns, hand grenades and bombs.

During the Third Battle of Ypres in the summer of 1917 the *Schustas* were heavily engaged in harassing Allied troops. Unfortunately they were still flying two-seater C types, as used by the *FA* and *FA (A)* units and their losses were heavy. During the summer they began to receive the first of the new CL types. These were lighter, faster and more manoeuvrable than the C type. Also new tactics were employed, with a flight of at least four machines attacking precise targets based on specific orders from the staff. Accurate timing was of the essence, with the *Schustas* keeping the heads of defending infantry and artillery down to enable the German troops to advance. As already mentioned, these new tactics meant that during the Battle of Cambrai

Halberstadt CLII White 3 of *Schusta* 2.

in November and December 1917 the *Schustas* were an important contribution to the success of the German counter-offensive.

In March 1918, the 38 *Schustas* were re-named *Schlachtstaffeln (Schlastas)*, or battle sections, which was more in keeping with their offensive employment. The main types used by the *Schlastas* were the Halberstadt CLII and CIV, and the Hannover CLII, CLIII and CLIIIa.

Though faster and more manoeuvrable than the C type, the CL machines were still extremely vulnerable to ground fire, as they had no armour for the crew or protection for the fuel tank. On 22 May 1918 Sergeant Kurt Anders and his gunner *Unteroffizier* Hans Wenner of *Schlasta* 19 were operating between Abeele and Poperinghe when they were shot down by Allied machine-gun fire and killed. Though a number of Halberstadt CLIIs had been shot down on the Allied side of the lines, their machine was still the subject of a detailed examination. Allocated the number G/2 Bde/11 there was very little left of it, with only the rear fuselage and one wing being intact. Despite this, much was gleaned from the wreckage, including the unusual construction of the wing main spar.

With the Allied offensive in late summer 1918, the *Schlasta* machines were used more as two-seater fighters on escort work and in a defensive mode for their own troops.

By the end of the war the British had a dedicated armoured ground attack machine, the Sopwith Salamander, but it arrived too late to be used operationally. The Germans though had learned the lessons of ground support, as was amply demonstrated by their *Blitzkrieg* tactics of the Second World War.

Return to the ring road and turn right back to Ypres. This completes the third and final tour of *Airfields and Airmen: The Channel Coast*.

Conclusion

For those readers whose interest in First World War aviation may have been aroused by this present book I can recommend joining *Cross and Cockade International – The First World War Aviation Historical Society*. Since publication of *Airfields and Airmen: Cambrai* the membership secretary's address has changed to:

Membership Secretary
Cross and Cockade International
11 Francis Drive
Westward Ho!
EX39 1XE
e-mail: cci@blueyonder.co.uk
website: http://www.crossandcockade.com

I can also recommend *Over the Front*, the journal of The League of World War I Aviation Historians. Their membership secretary's address has also changed and is:

Membership Secretary
The League of World War 1 Aviation Historians
16820 25th Ave. N.
Plymouth
MN 55447-2228
USA
e-mail: membership@overthefront.com
website: http://www.overthefront.com

In addition, I am always interested in contacting First World War aviators or their relatives, whether they figure in the *Airfields and Airmen* series of books or not.

My e-mail address is:
oconnor@stonehousecottage.freeserve.co.uk.

Further Reading

A Selected Bibliography

The Jasta Pilots, Franks, Bailey, Duiven, Grub Street 1996.
Above the Lines, Franks, Bailey, Guest, Grub Street 1993.
Above the Trenches, Shores, Franks, Guest, Grub Street 1990.
Over the Front, Franks and Bailey, Grub Street 1992.
The Jasta War Chronology, Franks, Bailey, Duiven, Grub Street 1998.
Above Flanders Fields, W M Pieters, Grub Street 1998.
Flying Corps Headquarters 1914-18, Maurice Baring, William Heinemann 1930.
A Contemptible Little Flying Corps, McInnes and Webb, The London Stamp Exchange 1991.
Five Years in the Royal Flying Corps, J T B McCudden, The Aeroplane and General
    Publishing Co Ltd 1918.
Years of Combat, Sholto Douglas, Collins 1963.
An Airman Marches, H H Balfour, Hutchinson and Co 1933.
Flying and Soldiering, R R Money, Ivor, Nicholson and Watson 1936.
VCs of the First World War 1914, G Gliddon, Sutton Publishing Ltd 1994.
German Fighter Units 1914-May 1917, Alex Imrie, Osprey Publishing 1978.
For Valour, The Air VCs, Chaz Bowyer,William Kimber 1978.
Air of Battle, W M Fry, William Kimber and Co Ltd 1974.
Hawker VC, Tyrrel M Hawker, Mitre Press 1965.
The Sky Their Battlefield, Trevor Henshaw, Grub Street 1995.
Airmen Died in the Great War, Chris Hobson, Hayward and Son 1995.
Aviation Awards of Imperial Germany in World War 1 Vols 1 - 7, Neal W O'Connor,
    Foundation for Aviation World War 1, 1988 – 1999.
Pictorial History of the German Army Air Service, Alex Imrie, Ian Allan 1971.
The Fokker Triplane, Alex Imrie, Arms and Armour 1992.
Sopwith Scout 7309, P G Taylor, Cassell and Co 1968.
The Price of Honour, G L Rossano, USN Institute Press 1991.
Days on the Wing, Willy Coppens, John Hamilton Ltd 1932.
I Chose the Sky, L H Rochford, William Kimber and Co Ltd 1977.
Barker VC, Wayne Ralph, Grub Street 1997.
Wings over the Somme, G H Lewis, William Kimber and Co Ltd 1976.
Zeppelin! Ray Rimell, Conway Maritime Press Ltd 1984.
Against the Odds, W A Williams, Bridge Books 1989.
Fighter Pilot on the Western Front, E D Crundall, William Kimber and Co Ltd 1975.
Royal Naval Air Service 1912-1918, Brad King, Hikoki Publications 1997.
First Through the Clouds, F Warren Merriam, B T Batsford Ltd 1954.
Flight Path, F T Courtney, William Kimber and Co Ltd 1972.
Medal of Honour Aviators of World War One, Alan E Durkota, Flying Machines Press 1998.
The Storks, N Franks and F Bailey, Grub Street 1998.
Into the Blue, Norman Macmillan, Jarrolds 1969.
The Flying Camels, C G Jefford, Privately printed 1995.
Air Command, R Collishaw and R V Dodds, William Kimber and Co Ltd 1973.
Down the Flare-Path, D H Montgomery, John Hamilton 1937.
High Adventure, A H Cobby, Kookaburra Technical Publications Pty 1981.
The First Battle of Britain, R H Fredette, Cassell and Co Ltd 1966.
Hanriot HD1, Windsock Datafile No. 12, J M Bruce and R Rimell, Albatros
    Publications Ltd 1988.
Gotha! P Grosz, I R Stair, G H Merrill, R L Rimell, Albatros Publications Ltd 1994.
Handley Page Bombers of the First World War, Chaz Bowyer, Aston Publications 1992.
Van Pionier Tot Luchtridder, R Lampaert, Uitgeverij De Krijger 1997.
Luchtoorlog Boven West-Vlaanderen 1914-1918, Bernard Deneckere, Uitgeverij
    Groeninghe n.v. 1998.
The Zeebrugge and Ostend Raids 1918, D Lake, Pen and Sword Books Ltd 2004.
The Zeebrugge Raid, P Warner, William Kimber and Co Ltd 1978.

INDEX

208